WHICH WAY TO SCHOOL?

For my Wife

PHILIP MAY

Which Way to School?

LION PUBLISHING

LION PUBLISHING
29–33 Lower Kings Road, Berkhamsted, Herts

First edition October 1972

ISBN 0 85648 004 5 (Casebound)
0 85648 005 3 (Paperback)

Printed in Great Britain by
Hazell Watson & Viney Ltd,
Aylesbury, Bucks

CONTENTS

FOREWORD

Philip May is already well known for his research among teachers and pupils, much of which was reported and discussed in his book *Moral Education in School* (1971). Backed by this research, he now gives us a study of the underlying principles, not just of religious instruction as a school subject, but of the meaning of Christianity as an inspiration throughout education. He shows that the basic values accepted in Western education have been nourished in the Christian tradition and only fully make sense when understood in that context. He argues, not only that our education has developed historically in the Christian tradition, but that this same tradition can best illuminate our vision of education for the future.

This contribution to the study of education is most welcome at a time when research tends to be preoccupied with means rather than ends – a preoccupation which is not surprising in a civilization which is concerned with quantity rather than quality, whether it be measured in terms of the statistics of industrial output and export, the mileage of motorways constructed at enormous cost, the sales of pop records, or the number of 'A' levels achieved in the largest Comprehensive school.

Our preoccupation with quantity, and with means rather than ends, makes this book all the more timely. Christian educators in these days have much to contend with – not only the moral confusion of our permissive society, but the new aggressiveness of the secular humanists who would like to see religion cast out of the curriculum, and the bewilderment caused among the faithful by the 'New Theology'.

As well as fortifying Christian teachers, this book should

stimulate some salutary rethinking in those who have little use for the Christian tradition. It is to be hoped that the book will be read, not only by the converted, but by sceptics. Indifference and hostility towards Christian teaching comes less from people who have understood and rejected it than from those who have never understood.

M. V. C. Jeffreys
Emeritus Professor, University of Birmingham

PREFACE

Christians have always recognized the importance of education, and since New Testament times have been active in it, following Hebrew precedent. Yet while the Bible rightly plays an important part in the religious education given to our children in the nation's schools, specifically Christian thinking is not noticeably prominent in current educational discussions.

Such thinking – on any issue – has always derived its distinctively Christian emphasis from Biblical sources, and there is a great deal in the Old and New Testaments which bears upon educational theory and practice. Some of its ideas have been central to the educational philosophy of Western civilization for a very long time. But it seems that no attempt has ever been made to gather together all that it has to say which is relevant to the teaching situation. It might be especially appropriate therefore, at a time when society in general is becoming less and less familiar with Biblical concepts, to consider this teaching afresh.

The point is not being argued that in every sphere of learning and teaching Christian doctrine has definite and distinctive educational comments to make. In many technical and administrative matters, opinion and practice are not in any way directly dependent upon the religious beliefs of those involved. Decisions should be taken either on purely empirical and logical grounds or on the basis of practical expediency. It would, however, be wrong to assume that Christian teaching has nothing specific to contribute. Many of the assumptions made by English educationists – about the nature, needs and rights of children, about the aims and content of education, about standards and values in education – owe a great deal to Christian teaching and Christian action. Some people today might be surprised to discover the real source of basic educational attitudes that they cherish.

This book does not attempt a full survey of today's educational and social problems. What it simply tries to do is to examine the Biblical teaching which can legitimately be applied to the educational sphere. This teaching is scattered throughout the Old and New Testaments and is rarely presented in systematic or concentrated form. But it is consistent, clear, and in certain points detailed. The pages that follow try to set out this teaching and to show its permanent application to education. It is hoped that this will encourage others to reconsider educational ideas and practical problems in the light of the Bible, and to take further some of the basic principles outlined here, so helping teachers and administrators to see educational issues in a Christian perspective.

In this connection the author wishes to acknowledge, with grateful thanks, all the help he has received down the years from members of the Association of Christian Teachers and the former Christian Education Fellowship. Their encouragement, guidance and stimulus to thinking have been invaluable.

Chapter One

TOWARDS BETTER EDUCATION

To an outside observer the current educational scene must appear somewhat confused. Considerable energy is certainly being expended in many directions, for instance on the problems of the primary school, and on secondary reorganization. Many projects are exploring new ideas and methods in curriculum development. Research goes on into questions of testing and examining at various levels. Much thought is being given to ways of expanding universities and other further education facilities. The sheer range of the field is so great that it would be difficult to obtain a coherent picture of it in any case. But the task is complicated by the fact that so much disagreement exists among the experts as to ways and means in education, and is made more formidable by the publicity which such disagreement receives.

This helps to explain why most of those concerned in education are reluctant even to try to assess the total picture, or to determine exactly where current activity will lead. It seems more practical simply to concentrate on one's own small part. We are like a field commander who has become so involved in the problems and tactics of the immediate battle that he neglects the over-all strategy of the war, and may even have forgotten why it is being fought.

We are right, of course, to be concerned about the immediate present. And analyses of the current educational scene, such as the Crowther, Albemarle, Newsom, Robbins and Plowden Reports, have been most valuable. But like Gideon's crack brigade who kept a sharp eye on the enemy as they drank, we need to consider the real task that confronts us, as well as our immediate circumstances. Now although there is a good deal of contemporary literature on aims in education, we do not really seem to be sure in which direction real progress lies. True, we know that our campaign is for a better standard of education for everyone. A great deal of emphasis at the moment is being placed on the provision of better buildings, more up-to-date and efficient equipment, more appropriate curricula and more well-qualified and well-trained staff. We are undertaking a reorganization of the whole system from the nursery school upwards. And the assumption underlying all this appears to be that once this has been achieved – once we possess all these superior schools and teachers, and the system has had time to settle down – then *everything* will be better.

But what is 'better'? Perhaps there will be greater equality of opportunity. It will be splendid if more chances become available for all our pupils to progress as far as they can, and to gain all the qualifications they need. Our modern technological society demands that our children have more time at school and a better education than we did. We desire all this for them not merely so that they can help to operate the country's machinery, but so that they can cope at all with the complications of modern life. Perhaps the teacher's path will be made smoother. Educational research has been giving teachers more encouragement lately. Successful efforts are now being made to plan stimulating courses of study, and effective ways of teaching this material to children of all ages have been suggested. The best of these courses and methods not only recognize the demands of the subject concerned, but are also more closely geared to the nature and needs of the individual pupils. The teaching of our children and young people may well become more efficient, so that they will reap the maximum benefit from their time at school and college. Much more, of course, needs to be done, and shortage of money frustrates many developments, but it is good that time, money and thought are being spent upon our children.

What is 'better'? This question needs much thought, and the financial restrictions we sometimes find frustrating will in fact be useful if they give us pause for thought. It is also a question easier to answer in terms of buildings and techniques than in terms of people. That is probably why so many of us concentrate on the educational environment rather than on the individuals who throng it. Yet when we do consider the pupils in the system as well as just the system itself, do we not find, in fact, whatever our disclaimers, that we are only really aiming to create experts – men and women specially equipped in limited areas to construct tools or to use them? To put the question like this may overstate the case, but there is too much truth in it for comfort. We are producing specialists, whether they are to operate in the factory, the company office, or the university and government research departments. The whole educational system is being increasingly geared to this end. The less able must be made more able, and the talented more talented still. Being average is not good enough any more. So the pressures increase, on teachers and taught alike. These pressures have become so intense that it is probably true to say that many of those involved in education rarely if ever think about the end product of all this effort. There is simply not the time. So where *should* we be aiming?

Much of the emphasis in education today is misplaced. Our vision is blurred. We cannot see the wood for the trees. What education should most be concentrating upon, as the Newsom Report underlined, and as many individual teachers hold in practice, is the children as persons. We should primarily be thinking of them as future adults, parents and citizens rather than as potentially skilled technicians for industry, commerce, the civil service or teaching. To argue in this way is not to attack the careers guidance and counselling activities which many schools undertake. Such work is an essential part of the programme of every secondary school, and in most schools it could be extended, with profit to all concerned. Still less is this viewpoint to be seen as part of that wave of anti-intellectualism currently beating against the doors of those who uphold what is often called 'grammar school education'. We need to beware of making our pupils specialize too early and too much, yet our abler young people must be initiated into specialist academic study before they leave school. Nevertheless the *main* stress in education today should be on character, not calling, on living rather than learning.

Perhaps it is unfair to suggest that personal development is talked about but largely neglected in practice. The growth of child-centred teaching, especially in primary schools, is certainly a hopeful sign. And what about that popular current topic, moral education? Surely personality development and pupil welfare attract much attention now. Does not the growing concern over the moral education of young people refute the view that we give too little attention to the idea of character training in schools today? This concern is indeed welcome. The danger is that it will merely result in one more compartment on school timetables. Special periods for moral education are favoured by a majority of teachers and of 14–16 year old pupils (according to recent nationwide surveys),[1] and could be of great value.

Yet we can too easily assume that just because we set aside time in school to examine ethical principles and discuss practical moral problems, the pupils will not only be better equipped to face life but will themselves be better people. The first part of the assumption may well be correct. The second is not. That ignorance is the cause of folly and that once pupils are more knowledgeable they will behave more responsibly just is not true. Knowledge does not necessarily bring wisdom and rectitude.

It is dangerous, too, to follow blindly the creed which propounds that all moral issues should be brought out into the open because the children may well have to know some time. It is dangerous because it is based on an inadequate, unrealistic view of man, and it fails to consider adequately the needs of developing young people, not all of whom are always able to cope with 'all the facts'. If we are to take moral education seriously, we must review the whole of our teaching, not just add one more subject to the timetable. To give character training its due priority in practice means that content and methods, and educational administration, need to be revised so that this priority is felt in all we do. More important still, we need again at this point real vision of the nature and potential of man.

Wisdom, knowledge, skills are indeed vital at the individual and national levels. But those who acquire this learning are more vital still. 'People matter more than things.' The past has much to teach us at this point. Educational philosophers and practitioners alike from Plato onwards stress the chief end of education as being the development of the 'good' or 'virtuous' man. 'Education in virtue from youth upwards, which makes a man eagerly pursue the ideal perfection of citizenship, and teaches him how rightly to rule and how to obey . . . is the only education which . . . deserves the name,' said Plato in *The Laws*.[2] Erasmus argued that the main function of education 'is that the tender spirit may drink in the seeds of piety'.[3] Comenius believed that the main issues of our life in this world are 'learning, virtue and piety'.[4] Locke pronounced that 'the great business of all is virtue and wisdom',[5] whilst Herbart's view was that 'the one and whole work of education may be summed up in the concept – Morality'.[6] Many similar sentiments could be quoted from other educationists and writers on the subject. They did not necessarily agree about the best methods to achieve their aims, nor were all their presuppositions about man always the same. They nonetheless put people before skills and life before aspects of living.

In the last analysis everything depends on one's view of man. If man is naturally innocent and good then a better environment – be it new schools, new teaching techniques based on the latest psychological understanding of the nature of the learning process, or new syllabuses – will achieve the progress desired. But the very fact that there is emphasis today on the need for moral education shows that many are beginning to recognize that a more satisfactory environment is not enough. Yet so many teachers are confused about proper standards that they are reluctant even to appear to be setting themselves up before their pupils as authorities on moral issues. It is safer to burrow in the warren of specialist study. The critics of our nation's traditional standards strive to knock down, but offer no coherent alternative system, no set of values and ideals which may be generally accepted. This is exactly where Christianity can give an answer to the educationist's dilemma.

The one supreme, authoritative record of Christian teaching, as the stated confessions of all the major Christian denominations underline, is the Bible. To this source book all who are concerned with education may turn with profit. In the Old and New Testaments there is not only plenty of useful material for moral education lessons but a realistic and detailed view of the origin, nature and destiny of man. The Bible has much to say about children and parents, and about social relationships. There is a great deal concerning the created order and the purpose of life, and about wisdom, knowledge and cultural gifts. As one progresses through the various writings, the development of thought on many of these issues becomes clearer. A good illustration of this, as a later chapter will show, is the subject of wisdom. Yet few writers of textbooks on education ever refer to the Biblical teaching that is relevant to their themes. In the pages that follow we shall try to fill this gap in the literature of education, and to consider those aspects of the Scriptural record which relate to educational matters. For Biblical teaching can provide us with basic principles and the highest standards, so that both our thinking and our practice in education may receive a new dynamic. Clear Christian thinking is much needed in the world of teaching and learning, as it is everywhere else. If applied, it would bring true perspective and real coherence to the multifarious activities of the day. In its practical down-to-earth way it would make the phrase 'better education' a meaningful term, and enable us to offer a better education for all.

Just over one hundred years ago the humanist T. H. Huxley wrote of the Bible: 'By the study of what other book could children be so much humanised?'[7] Since his day there has been much controversy about the historicity of the Bible. This argument still continues, although there appears to be an increasing return in theological scholarship to more conservative positions. Nevertheless, very real and honest disagreements exist about the meaning of the Bible and how it is 'inspired'. Professor D. M. Mackay has a useful comment to make here. In an article entitled 'Science and . . .', he suggested that 'the (ideal) scientific attitude of *reverence towards data* might well be inculcated more realistically towards Holy Scripture. It is not a matter of prejudging its validity, but rather of realizing the kind of approach demanded, in the nature of the case, if such data as it claims to offer are ever to be fairly evaluated. The unbiased scientist's question "What if it were true?" needs to be asked – and worked out in terms of attitude more often in the study of the Bible than it is today.'[8]

This is not the place to examine the many problems of Biblical interpretation. The Bible as a whole claims that God reveals himself – in both words and deeds. He directs and orders redemptive history and also has inspired a written account of that history. And it is God who enlightens men and women in every age to honour the authority of this revelation as they grasp its significance for themselves and for all mankind. All the Biblical writers assume that men can only know God if he first discloses himself. We should never, by studying the life of Christ or God's works in history, know that he is God and that they are his works if he had not spoken to make these things clear to us. 'Thus saith the Lord', the Scriptures say. We read that they are 'written for our instruction' and 'profitable for doctrine, reproof, correction and instruction in righteousness'. They are true, a sure guide, and as Christ himself asserted, they are permanent and cannot be broken.[9]

This historical revelation was given gradually and one can trace the development of thought through the Old and then the New Testaments. Each generation of people has to learn its truth afresh for itself. Religious experience is progressive, like all experience. The Jewish people, as the Old Testament records, had a growing sense of being a people set apart, chosen for a special destiny. Up to Roman times they clung to the illusion that God had selected them to play a triumphant role in history by bringing about, with his help, God's kingdom on earth. The New Testament revelation showed that their role was very different. It took Christ's closest followers a long time to realize the true nature of his Messiahship. Then, as their writings show, they were led to understand the consistent, developing message which writer after writer in the Old Testament set forth.

The best interpreter of the Bible is the Bible itself. As Calvin succinctly noted: 'Scripture indeed is self-authenticated.'[10] Most Protestants have always affirmed that the gospel message can be understood by anyone who reads it prayerfully and with diligence. This is not to suggest that the study of this very diverse collection of literature is a simple, undemanding pastime. The Bible is not an open book, all of which is immediately clear to the ordinary reader. It does not always speak as directly to us as to the people for whom its words were originally written. It has a message for the modern world as for any other age, a message which speaks with real contemporary relevance. But unless a reader is prepared to familiarize himself with some of the findings of Biblical scholarship – unless, for example, he takes the trouble to examine the historical context of what he is reading – he will not find some parts very comprehensible. If he is not willing to spend much time in very careful study, he will not gain very much. Yet as this book hopes to show, an examination of Biblical teaching reveals a great deal that is applicable to the sphere of education.

A few of the basic terms used in the Bible to describe the teaching process are worth examining. Of a number of words and their derivatives used in the Hebrew, the two most common are *lamad* and *yasar*. The root meaning of both these terms is 'to discipline' or 'to chasten for corrective purposes'. *Lamad* and its related terms are the more frequent, and embedded in the heart of these words is the idea of some kind of set standard, or target to be aimed at. *Yasar*, on the other hand, includes the sterner side of discipline, in stressing rather the need for admonition and reproof. In the Greek of the New Testament, though several terms are used, two again are most prominent: *didasko*, which may fairly be said to correspond to the Hebrew *lamad*, means 'to teach, to enable to learn, know, understand', and *paideuo*, which is nearer to *yasar*, means 'to rear, teach, discipline the young'.

The Biblical writings proclaim a standard which we are exhorted to teach as clearly as possible. They also stress that the natures of our pupils need to be corrected to enable them to reach that standard. Proverbs 22 : 6 effectively sums up these ideas: 'Train up a child in the way he should go', says the writer, 'and when he is old he will not depart from it.' He draws attention to the power and influence for good which properly directed education can have upon the young. The writer particularly has in mind the child's parents, and it is their opportunity and duty which are being underlined. The Hebrew word translated 'train' literally means 'dedicate'. Each child's upbringing should accord with the manner of life we desire our children to adopt. Implicit in these words, therefore, are the meanings: 'direct the child in the right, true way' and 'guide the child in the way best suited to his individual nature and needs'. Implicit also is the belief that teaching should begin early when the mind of the child is still impressionable.

Consequently this verse provides us with a perfectly balanced statement which emphasizes the importance of the highest standards, of individual needs, of the duty of teaching, and of right goals. It corrects the past over-insistence on standards without real consideration of the children being taught, and also the present tendency here and there to overstress the need for 'child-centred education' with too little regard for subject-matter or for absolute standards. The idea of 'dedication' reminds us of the crucial significance of the whole business of learning and teaching. No writer on education since has given a neater or a better summary of the teacher's task.

REFERENCES TO CHAPTER ONE

1 See P. R. May, 'Teachers' Attitudes to Moral Education', *Educational Research*, Vol. II, No. 3, June 1969, pp. 215–218. Also see P. R. May, *Moral Education in*

School, Methuen, 1971, for fuller accounts of the research surveys plus detailed discussion of the whole subject.

2 Plato, *The Laws* (trans. B. Jowett), Book I, OUP, 1953, p. 209.

3 Erasmus, *De Civilitate Morum Puerilium*.

4 J. A. Comenius, *The Great Didactic* (trans. and ed. M. W. Keatinge), A. & C. Black, 1923, p. 39.

5 John Locke, in J. W. Adamson, *The Educational Writings of John Locke*, OUP, 1922, p. 168.

6 J. F. Herbart, *The Science of Education*, Swan Sonnenschein, 1904, p. 57.

7 From his essay in the *Contemporary Review*, Vol. XVI, No. 1, December 1870, quoted in C. Bibby, *T. H. Huxley, Scientist, Humanist and Educator*, C. A. Watts, 1959, p. 152.

8 D. M. Mackay, 'Science and . . .', in *Religion in Education*, Vol. 27, No. 1, Autumn 1959, p. 22.

9 Romans 15: 4; 2 Timothy 3: 16; John 17: 17; Psalm 119: 105; Matthew 24: 35; 5: 18; John 10: 35.

10 John Calvin, *Institutes of the Christian Religion*, ed. J. T. McNeill, SCM Press, 1961, Book I, chapter 7, section 5, p. 80.

Chapter Two

THE RELEVANCE OF CHRISTIAN TEACHING TO EDUCATION

No one has ever been able to invent a really satisfying definition of the word 'education', though many have made brave attempts to do so. Most people, however, would agree about what we should include under this term. Education involves the whole person, and that means the physical, mental and spiritual growth and development to maturity of every child. Certain ingredients are essential to such progress. For instance there is information that man has accumulated about himself and his history. Children need to understand their immediate environment, and the society and world in which they live. Then also instruction and practice must be given in various skills and techniques. We hope to pass on certain standards, values, ideas and beliefs, concerning God and man, purpose and conduct, social living, science, literature and the arts. Each new generation is initiated into acceptable ways of living, social customs, and group habits and mores. It is therefore the values, principles and general outlook of each society which determine the kind and content of its children's education. For instance, anthropologists in recent years have been describing the simple, clear ritual introduction to adult status and responsibility which adolescents in primitive societies receive at the age of 12, 13 or 14. This contrasts sharply with the much more prolonged and complex experience of the twentieth-century adolescent who is not finally deemed to be a fully responsible adult, in Britain at least, until he is 18 years old.

Two main considerations lie at the heart of the Western educational systems: the good of the individual and the good of society.

The one concerns the development and well-being of the individual child. It is a preoccupation with personal welfare – comfort, security, competence and happiness – and with self-improvement. As the Newsom Report expresses it, children should be helped 'to develop their full capacities for thought and taste and feeling'.[1] The other emphasizes social welfare, the progress and betterment of society as a whole – 'to fit children', in the words of the Plowden Report, 'for the society into which they will grow up.'[2] In this connection the aim is to raise standards of living, and to increase the understanding and mastery of man's environment. So the basis of educational reform, in trying to improve the quality of the education we provide and to increase educational opportunity at all levels, is that we should cater both for the welfare of each child and for the community as a whole.

The assumption is that as we educate more efficiently, so we shall inevitably progress towards self-betterment and greater all-round happiness. A typical statement of this attitude is that of scientific humanists who, according to J. A. Lauwerys, believe that 'the chief instrument for the achievement of a better society is the right kind of school and the right kind of learning'.[3] H. L. Elvin has more recently said much the same thing. He very reasonably states that 'we should all agree that the maintenance of what is good in our present society, as well as the possibility of its improvement in (various) directions, will depend very much on education'.[4] His belief in the power of education to bring about 'the vigorous renewal of our national life'[5] colours the whole of his interesting book. James Hemming keeps reiterating his view that 'every person grown straight in the strength of his own spirit through the experience of a good personal and social education is a surety of peace and progress'.[6] The sociologist J. B. Mays frequently writes about his belief that education is a major influence for the guidance of social change, change which he believes will improve the quality of individual and group life and relationships.[7] Most of us take it for granted that education is essential to the enrichment of the individual and of the society in which he lives, although we might believe that the right kind of home is even more important than 'the right kind of school'. Yet before accepting these attractive opinions without further thought, we need to be aware of the presuppositions which lie behind them. They seem to assume that education somehow has the power in its very processes to create better people, so that the educated man and woman will always be superior, intellectually, morally and socially, to the uneducated. They further imply certain beliefs about the nature of man and about the purpose of life, which will be considered in a subsequent chapter.

Since education in any society involves the guiding and moulding of the young, it is an ethical undertaking. It should therefore be based on some sort of system of ultimate convictions, in particular convictions about man and the life he should lead. For our view of man, and what we consider to be the point of his existence, will determine both what we teach our children and how we do it. If we conceive that his role in life is to be the servant of the state, one who works principally for the common good, then we shall doubtless want him to be as technically skilled as possible, respectful and obedient to authority, a good 'organization man'. If we see his purpose in life to be self-fulfilment, we shall encourage him to develop and express his personality, and we shall emphasize the values of individuality, self-development and personal well-being. Whatever our attitude, we can turn to various sources for help as we try to achieve a balanced, rounded view of man's nature and potential, and of his situation. Educationists today usually rely upon four main aids. One is psychology, man's study of man. Another is sociology, the study of man in his social environment. Then there is our cultural heritage, man's accumulated storehouse of wisdom and experience down the ages. The fourth is philosophy, in which man attempts to examine his ideas and values and to arrive at satisfactory foundations on which to base his judgments and practice.

Unquestionably, from all four of these sources we learn a great deal, and as understanding grows and research techniques improve, we should extend our knowledge in all these areas and make more precise use of it. Even in a general way we can see that the effectiveness of every teacher's personal relationships with his pupils and the success of the teaching methods he employs depend very much upon his understanding of children's physical and mental growth, behaviour patterns, how they learn, the problems of adolescence, and so on. Educational psychology is an essential aid. All teachers need a clear grasp of the relationships between home and school in their area, the nature of the environment from which their pupils come, and the claims which society in general is making upon its members. Sociology comes in when we try to determine the nature and historical background of our educational institutions, and to comprehend the part played by the state at any given time in the sphere of education. To understand the role of the state is particularly vital for educational administrators, since the state will influence so much of their work. We can see also that the content of education along with new developments in the curriculum will be greatly affected by the teachers' insight into human values and their regard for cultural traditions. Finally, teachers should be able to justify and evaluate their work, and give an account of the principles which lie behind what they do. We all need to be aware of the basic beliefs which form the source and ground of our conduct. We need also to be able to distinguish between truth and opinion – between facts which remain true and unalterable regardless of what anybody thinks about them, and truths which may present different facets to different people. It would not do to lead pupils either into credulous dogmatism, or into unbridled scepticism. Teachers in particular should be able to sort out the value judgments which we all weave into our educational discussions. Some training in philosophical analysis and the study of educational theory is therefore of real importance. However, when all this has been said, it is not the task of the philosopher, psychologist or sociologist to dictate to the teacher, but only to help him.

Now psychology, sociology, cultural studies and philosophy

all have one and the same basic limitation, because of which they cannot give us that complete understanding of the nature of man and the purpose of life which we would need in order to evolve and justify from first principles a reasoned theory of education. For none of these studies can ever be completely objective. Man by himself is unable to climb out of himself so that he can view himself and his world from outside. Although these 'proper studies' provide us with much vital information and many illuminating insights, the picture they paint remains inevitably incomplete. Some people – among educationists, D. J. O'Connor, for instance[8] – would defend human reason as a perfectly adequate objective instrument to assess and interpret all things. Harry Blamires, however, has pointed out that 'to proclaim human reason fit to generalize about data derived from observation of phenomena (e.g. that Nature is uniform) is to assert that human reason has an intrinsic validity exalting it above that other created matter and created life which it observes'.[9] He goes on to argue that human reason can have this validity only if divinely created and not blindly evolved, since if it is only a meaningless product of evolution its judgments and generalizations are also meaningless.

To believe that man's reason can ultimately explain and interpret everything else is an act of faith in man's self-sufficiency, in man's reason as the absolute authority. Such faith asserts that man is completely capable of determining who and what he is, and that his future is entirely in his own hands. Yet reason is only a part of human nature. As Herman Dooyeweerd has stated, 'human reason is not an independent substance; much rather is it an instrument. The *I* is the hidden player who avails himself of this instrument'.[10] He claims that men try to 'absolutize what has only a relative and dependent existence'.[11] For philosophical thought is as much bound to the temporal order of human experience as is the study of the natural sciences. R. J. Rushdoony comments fairly when he exclaims that to 'absolutize one aspect of creation is to distort all of creation'.[12]

If man, or man's reason, is the measure of all things, then absolute standards as the Christian thinks of them cease to exist. Certain secular humanists, in fact, would deny that standards can be anything but relative. Sir Julian Huxley has declared that any belief in absolutes erects a formidable barrier against progress and the possibility of improvement in the moral, rational or religious spheres.[13] He and others like-minded believe that ethical values will change as time passes, and they talk of man's progress as though this is inevitable. How we can measure this advancement against purely relative standards we are never told. To know how far we have travelled along the road, we must have a fixed destination in view. Indeed, standards which are true and permanent provide not barriers but spurs to progress, offering as they do goals at which to aim. The humanist is therefore in a cleft stick. Man must, in his view, set himself up as the authority to whom all appeals must be made. Yet our nature is such that we cannot ever be completely sure of ourselves.

This poses very real practical problems for the teacher, especially when his authority is called into question, by sceptical adolescents for instance. Should teachers proclaim their standards and values as the best they know? How do they themselves, let alone their pupils, cope with the insecurity they must feel in a climate of thought in which certainty about beliefs and ideals, about what is excellent or worthless, cannot logically be present? How far are they arbiters of right and wrong in the child's world? How can they convince their pupils that ideals such as hard work, honesty, the love of beauty and consideration for others are worth serious attention, especially if the environment in which the children live openly contradicts such teaching? Some values are relative for the Christian as for the humanist, in that they depend on the basic values. But if everything is relative, why should pupils respect certain standards merely because an adult calls them 'better' even if they admire that adult? The task is difficult enough in any case. If there are no standards, no absolutes, or if fallible man is the supreme authority, it becomes well-nigh impossible. In such a world, young people will not contest and reject the teacher's authority occasionally or sporadically. They will do it constantly and inevitably.

Such a challenge to authority is a difficulty which confronts not only the teaching profession. All authority – of the church, the state, the law, parents – is being increasingly questioned. The uncertainty which these attacks are creating in the minds of many people in all walks of life is reflected in that loss of central purpose in work which Spencer Leeson noted in his Bampton lectures on Christian Education.[14] He stressed that many things were now becoming, both in the world and in education, ends in themselves, where he believed they had no such right. Particular examples he gave were knowledge, power and happiness. If such are the goals of education, we have a duty to investigate whether they are proper goals, and ask by what right they have been set up. The trouble is that in a world of relative values everyone has the right to set up goals, and to question the authority of every other person who tries to do so. Every departure will be greeted with distrust by someone. There are no universals to help explain the particulars, as Francis Schaeffer puts it.[15] Consequently, if man is dependent solely upon himself in this situation, all that our society can do in its educational theory and practice is – to borrow a phrase from an American writer – 'to recreate the child in its own image'.[16]

It is in just this situation, where all values seem relative, where the authority of man has no ultimate foundation, where the purpose of life is uncertain and where man's self-knowledge is too fragmentary to provide a sure basis for working convictions, that the Christian message is clear and distinctive. Some years ago, G. H. Bantock pointed out that a most urgent problem not just for education but for our whole society is to find 'an authority . . . that will allow man to come to his true "self"'. And this, he says, 'in the last resort is what education implies'.[17] Christians believe that Christianity holds the key to this very problem. For the Christian gospel goes beyond what the humanist can say, in that in Christ and Christian theology there is the why and the wherefore of all true standards and values.

The Christian religion maintains that God is absolute, and that he created the universe in which we live, and ourselves in it. He is, moreover, all-powerful, all-knowing, all-wise and absolutely good, and created all things in such a way that they are perfect in so far as their relationship with him is perfect. This means that man can enjoy a personal relationship with him – for he is no remote and aloof deity – and that it is in so doing that he becomes truly man. It is through fellowship with God that true self-knowledge becomes possible. As John Calvin once said, 'it is certain that man never achieves a clear knowledge of himself unless he has first looked upon God's face, and then descends from contemplating Him, to scrutinize himself.'[18]

It follows from all this that Christian teaching has a relevance to the educational situation which should not be overlooked. Those who reject the Christian faith have to accept other 'authorities', such as self, power, reason, or the consensus of expert or mass opinion. All these fail the ultimate tests of objectivity and consistency, since man cannot escape from his situation in order to judge himself impartially. Furthermore his ideas and opinions change from time to time. If a country's education service is to set up true standards, provide right goals and have real purpose, there should be a coherent world view undergirding all the planning and teaching that takes place. It may not often be necessary in educational discussion and activity to refer or appeal to such a view. But its presence at the heart of all educational thinking would be there to provide stability and meaning to the whole enterprise.

Only Christianity offers this truly all-embracing and realistic world picture. In saying this, it is necessary to add that it is possible to recognize in theory the relevance of orthodox Christian teaching to education without assenting to the tenets of the Christian faith. Christianity offers detailed teaching about the person and will of the Creator, and his over-all purpose for life, along with much clear teaching about what attitudes one should adopt towards oneself, to others, to work, to possessions, to the world, to power and authority, to life in society, and above all to God himself. Thus it provides a framework on which to build, as well as a measure against which to test all other ideals and attitudes.

To argue that Christian teaching is relevant to the study of education in this way will certainly provoke the accusation of prejudice or bias. It might be thought that a person's religious beliefs are irrelevant or inappropriate to the business of learning and teaching. The argument that religion is irrelevant to education can only arise if we deny that education is concerned with the whole personality. Religious beliefs might be inappropriate in educational discussion if religious faith was simply something personal, private, an individual matter only. But religious belief is never something to be confined within one's own secret conscience. Everybody has certain basic presuppositions which they carry with them into everything they do. These assumptions colour their approach to educational as to any other issues which concern them. There is nothing wrong or foolish in this, nor will their attitudes or decisions be thereby automatically invalidated. What is important is that everyone concerned should be clear and open about the beliefs which motivate them to think and act as they do.

Inevitably the pupils who leave our schools will to some extent at least have been moulded by the educational system. Although the most powerful influence upon them is always the home, how they think, the values they hold, the way they behave, the goals at which they aim, their attitudes to themselves, to others and to life have all partly been shaped by the education they have received. Their schooling has determined much of their quality, and also some of their limitations in outlook and ability. We have helped to create what they are. If this is so, our fundamental beliefs about human nature and life on earth are crucial, for they assist us to determine what we teach and why. Education is not a neutral business. Our very belief in its importance declares our bias. Most of us want our children to share this opinion, just as we hope they will come – unforced – to believe in personal integrity, respect for others, considerate behaviour and responsible living. Such values are supplied not by philosophy, psychology, sociology or the subjects we teach in school but by our over-all view of man and the nature of life. Their origin is religious. They arise from those fundamental assumptions which constitute our faith concerning humanity and purpose in life. Christian teaching is, at the very least therefore, as relevant as any other set of basic beliefs in helping us to arrive at our educational ideals and practice.

Just as we saw in the previous chapter that moral education is not just a matter of adding another lesson to the timetable, in the same way for education to have a Christian perspective would not merely mean that school timetables should include religious knowledge lessons and acts of worship. Such activities may in fact be the only regular occasions when explicit reference is made to Christian teaching and practice, but the whole approach to children could also be informed by Christian understanding of human beings, their nature, powers, tasks and destiny. Indeed in Britain this is to some extent already the case more than we realize. Most of the standards and values we cherish in education are Christian in origin. Our attitudes to children and our high regard for education itself spring more from Christian influence than from any other source. It is a pity that this debt which our education owes to Christianity is in danger of being forgotten, as Christian standards have in the past been taken so much for granted. It seems to be assumed that they will always automatically influence our approach. Most people, for instance, would accept as fundamental those social principles of 'fairness, freedom, consideration for people's interests and respect for persons' which R. S. Peters has enumerated.[19] Our present understanding of what these terms mean is still largely determined by a Christian interpretation, but each new generation will continue to enjoy and apply such understanding only if men's minds are constantly refreshed by the Christian view of men and things. Values which originally took their significance from a particular ethical way of life will eventually become meaningless if that way of life dies out of our thinking.

Christian teaching has had great influence in the past on educational thinking and practice in England, as the early church schools, the seventeenth- and eighteenth-century nonconformist academies and many of the nineteenth-century public schools all bear witness. Such influence is still evident today. Yet if Christianity is rejected, it is arguable that no one can then be sure that our children will even continue always to be educated as human beings. The Christian element an perspective is necessary in our educational system for *all* children, for their own good. For it helps to guarantee that they will all, the ablest, the less able, the educationally sub-normal and the handicapped, continue to be treated with the respect and care which are their due as human beings. Without it, as the recent history of Germany under the Nazis and of certain East European countries has shown, education may easily degenerate into exploitation or unfair discrimination. A society which genuinely holds a Christian view of man will not promote the education of the intelligent at the expense of the dull and backward, or vice versa. It will not treat some children as fodder for factory and field and others as an élite to be given all the privileges which stem from skilled teaching and the finest facilities. Nor will it favour the children of one social class, ethnic group or particular creed to the detriment of children from other sections of the community.

How would a Christian perspective in education affect our teaching in practice? Let us take an analogy from literature. C. S. Lewis, in his essay on 'Christianity and Literature',[20] points out that there are no distinctive literary peculiarities attaching to works we call 'Christian literature'. The rules for writing are the same whatever the subject, and success in sacred literature depends on the same qualities which secure success in secular literature. Similarly, one can say that there are no specific rules for Christian education (as distinct from 'secular education' or even 'religious education') – nothing specifically Christian, that is, about the techniques of teaching. One does not use audio-visual methods in teaching a foreign language, or helpful laboratory procedures in teaching science, because of one's religious beliefs; nor films, drama and discussion in teaching the humanities because of one's religious convictions. These and any other appropriate teaching methods would be used in order to make a success of the work of teaching.

To return to the words 'Christian literature' for another parallel: a book may be felt to be Christian whatever its subject. We can sometimes feel that a book or speech is the work of a Christian, or a man sympathetic towards Christianity, because of the very attitude and atmosphere inherent in it. Similarly in education, it would be the basic attitude to teaching and to the subject taught which would be most significant. Today we find in education the same 'disquieting contrast' which C. S. Lewis found in his own field between 'the whole circle of ideas used in modern criticism and certain ideas recurrent in the New Testament'. This contrast he felt to be not so much the 'logical contradiction between clearly defined concepts' as 'a repugnance of atmospheres, a discordance of notes, an incompatibility of temperaments'.[21] It was with such contrasts in mind that Lewis suggested that there is a case for a Christian approach to literature, and one can similarly argue for a Christian approach to education.

With many of the problems of educational theory and practice it cannot be maintained that there are solutions open only to Christians. It may, however, be true to say that there are some solutions which can be derived only from ultimate Christian foundations. Many non-Christians show understanding and wisdom in educational situations – the fruit of long experience, wide reading and careful analysis – but they may not have thought through to the bases on which they act. It is argued elsewhere in this book that the underlying principles of respect for personality, truth and integrity are rooted in the Christian view of man. It is doubtful if they can be derived from any other source. Many teachers who would not call themselves Christians act upon these principles without feeling called upon to justify them. Christians will co-operate with them, and may not necessarily expect to import any fresh principles into the situation. If they introduce anything, it is simply the strengthened conviction which a knowledge of the foundations of those principles provides. Nevertheless Christian insight can shed light upon our educational thinking, and Christian values guide our practice. So we may be helped to ensure that what we do is in accord with a true world view and with the highest standards known to man.

REFERENCES TO CHAPTER TWO

1 *Half Our Future* (The Newsom Report), HMSO, 1963, p. 27.
2 *Children and their Primary Schools* (The Plowden Report), HMSO, 1967, Vol. I, p. 185.
3 J. A. Lauwerys, 'Scientific Humanism', in A. V. Judges, ed., *Education and the Philosophic Mind*, Harrap, 1957, p. 156.
4 H. L. Elvin, *Education and Contemporary Society*, C. A. Watts, 1965, p. 111.
5 *Ibid.*, p. 182.
6 James Hemming, *Teach Them to Live*, Longmans Green & Co., 1957, p. 2.
7 See, for instance, J. B. Mays, *The School in its Social Setting*, Longmans Green & Co., 1967.
8 See D. J. O'Connor, *An Introduction to the Philosophy of Education*, Routledge and Kegan Paul, 1957.
9 H. Blamires, *Repair the Ruins*, G. Bles, 1950, p. 20.
10 H. Dooyeweerd, *In the Twilight of Western Thought*, Presbyterian and Reformed Publishing Co., 1960, p. 192.
11 *Ibid.*, p. 118.
12 *Ibid.*, Introduction, p. xii.
13 Sir Julian Huxley, *The Humanist Frame*, Allen and Unwin, 1961.
14 S. Leeson, *Christian Education*, Bampton Lectures for 1944, published by Longmans Green and Co., 1947, pp. 110–111.
15 F. Schaeffer, *The God Who is There*, Hodder and Stoughton, 1968.
16 R. J. Rushdoony, *Intellectual Schizophrenia*, Presbyterian and Reformed Publishing Co., 1960, p. 127.
17 G. H. Bantock, *Freedom and Authority in Education*, Faber & Faber, 1952, p. 183.
18 J. Calvin, *Institutes of the Christian Religion*, ed. J. T. McNeill, SCM Press, 1961, Book I, Chapter 1, p. 37.
19 R. S. Peters, 'The status of social principles and objectives in a changing society', in *The Educational Implications of Social and Economic Change*, Schools Council Working Paper No. 12, HMSO, 1967, p. 31.
20 C. S. Lewis, 'Christianity and Literature', reprinted in *Christian Reflections*, G. Bles, 1967, pp. 1–3.
21 *Ibid.*

Chapter Three

AIM AND PURPOSE IN EDUCATION

A favourite pastime of educationists during the last fifty years or so has been to argue about aims in education. Various slogans have been advocated to help intending teachers to understand the purpose of their work. Recently, however, old disputes have been allowed to rest, and discussion has centred more upon differences of procedure. This change in direction is almost entirely due to the writings of Professor R. S. Peters. During the last decade, he has been reiterating with force and clarity the view that 'many disputes about the aims of education are disputes about principles of procedure rather than about "aims" in the sense of objectives to be arrived at by taking appropriate means'.[1] He believes that education is a process of initiation, that 'most of the important things in education are passed on . . . by example and explanation,'[2] and that 'the model of means to ends is not remotely applicable to the transaction that is taking place'.[3]

Nevetheless, many of us automatically regard the school life of our children as a kind of assembly line on which the raw material is placed at about the age of five years and from which the well-rounded, well-equipped, virtually mature young adult emerges ten or more years later. Hence the language of those who describe school leavers as 'products of the educational system'. A somewhat similar attitude lies behind the much older idea of life at school as growth, with the young plants coming to full bloom, or bearing fruit, as they enter the adult world of work. All these images have their usefulness. They let us down when they suggest that the educational process is more or less successfully completed by the time the formal training of young people has ended.

This is not to say that education can have no legitimate objectives, nor to support the view of the American philosopher John Dewey in his assertion that 'the educational process has no end beyond itself; it is its own end'.[4] Dewey's objective may be helpful in so far as he implies that our capacity for learning and enrichment of personality should continue throughout life. Yet surely no man wishes persistently to pursue knowledge merely for its own sake, or to go on learning in order to go on learning. To accept Peters' idea of education as initiation is helpful, but we should also remember that there are such things as standards or goals towards which our pupils should aim. The standard of the New Testament is summed up in the command of Christ to 'be perfect', and the Bible suggests certain criteria by which to judge our attitudes and test our progress. The goal for Christians is maturity, the full development of one's personality and powers, not simply for the personal satisfaction that this brings, nor for the practical benefits that others may enjoy from one's employment of wisdom and skill in their service. These are very important reasons, but the principal end for Christians is to 'glorify God' – to live out what God has created men to be. The more mature one is, the more effectively one should be able to carry this out.

Obviously the period of formal education plays a major part in helping children to grow into responsible adults. With this purpose in mind, the whole educative enterprise ought to be coherent and unified. The various parts should form an over-all pattern. At the very least this means that teachers at different stages should be fully cognizant of what their colleagues are doing. University dons and college lecturers ought to know in some detail the aims, content and methods of the secondary schools from which their students come. There should be similarly close liaison between primary and secondary school teachers. But, more than all this, we should realize that intellectual, moral and spiritual development go together. They are really inseparable aspects of growth. When we think, perceive, desire and will, the whole person is involved. It is impossible, for example, to impart knowledge and encourage intellectual development without affecting the emotions and desires of the heart, or without influencing the will. To concentrate on only one aspect of a child's education in school, say the intellectual, and to neglect the moral and spiritual sides of his upbringing is to run the risk of warping his mind and heart. Such an education is unbalanced and therefore soon lacks coherence. We must teach our pupils not only to master certain knowledge and skills. They also need training in making value judgments and in taking decisions. We must educate the emotions and the psyche through the study of literature, music, art, social studies and in religious education. We must assist their moral development, increasing their awareness of moral issues and of the consequences of different actions and attitudes. Our pupils must learn to exercise responsibility. We should strive to educate the whole person. As Professor Jaarsma has commented, 'the whole child goes to school, and the whole child is involved in every learning activity'.[5]

Educational psychologists are thinking along the lines of the education of the whole person when they remind us that the main needs of children are for love and affection, security, recognition and, as they grow older, responsibility. In an environment where these needs are satisfied as far as possible, all our pupils should learn to think for themselves, to love and acquire truth and to enjoy what is beautiful and good. They should acquire the skills and knowledge necessary to success in all the tests and examinations which it is appropriate for them to take. We have other hopes for our children. These are summarized in certain familiar phrases which appear in the educational press and echo round teachers' conference halls. We want our children to 'be themselves', 'to realize their potential', and to 'gain self-fulfilment'. They should, by the time they are young adults, be 'able to stand on their own feet', and 'be independent and self-reliant', not least because in the end 'they are on their own'. We hope they will prove to be responsible, considerate and law-abiding.

It would not be unfair to ask the people who use these terms exactly what they take them to mean. And what do they mean to the children and young people to whom they are frequently addressed? What attitudes to life and to life's purpose lie behind them? Do they embody an adequate view of man? Do they provide a satisfactory basis for a philosophy of education? Most of us, like Matthew Arnold, certainly wish our children to see life steadily and to see it whole, and we rely heavily upon our education system to ensure that they acquire such vision. But the Christian sees that to try to impart this vision implies something extra. As well as trying to enable children to find a place in society where they can make an effective and personally satisfying contribution, the Christian would help them to understand the real meaning of life, as he finds it taught in the Bible. Such understanding would place the phrases quoted in the previous paragraph in a different light. To bring the Christian concept of maturity to bear upon such expressions renders them far more realistic. In Christianity there are no illusions about self-sufficiency or errors about 'aloneness'. Christian maturity is characterized by strength but not pride, humility and patience, a quiet mind, self-denying love of God and man, and an outlook governed by eternal perspectives that is full of certain hope, joy and confidence in Christ.

Education has always been necessary, from the beginning of man's life upon earth. His first mandate told him to be fruitful and to subdue the earth and have dominion over every living thing. If man is effectively to carry out these tasks of mastery and rule, he needs to learn much about himself and his environment. This inevitably involves him in study and in the transmitting of knowledge and wisdom from one generation to the next. Christians claim, however, that these things are not the whole of education. Man's chief task is to acknowledge and glorify God, and to make him known as he is found in his word, in nature and in history. In Bible times this task was performed by the parents and the church. Today the schools, with the teachers acting *in loco parentis*, share the responsibility for education and with it a responsibility towards God also.

We may now examine more closely some of the suggestions current today as to the purposes of education. A number are worth attention but they all need to be scrutinized with care. The fact that they seem reasonable, and command wide agreement in educational circles, does not mean that they should be accepted unquestioningly. From a Christian point of view they are sometimes inadequate or incomplete. The rest of this chapter will therefore consider some of the most popular suggestions in the light of Christian teaching about man and the purpose of life.

Early in his helpful little book *Education: an Introductory Survey*,[6] Professor W. O. Lester Smith lists four aims which are widely accepted by educationists. The first concerns the development of intelligence. Whitehead has defined education as 'the acquisition of the art of the utilisation of knowledge'[7] – learning to use knowledge. English educationists have always stressed this, and have realized how important is the development of each pupil's reasoning powers. They often associate this development, however, from the junior school stage to the university, with study of a mainly academic nature. On the other hand, everyone would agree that as many pupils as possible should be able to think clearly for themselves and to make detached judgments. We want them to have, in the words of a report on primary education, 'a proper sense of independence in thought and action, which implies a power to choose and to make judgments on their own account'.[8]

Let us consider some of the ideas we have here in the light of Christianity. The most fundamental of these is the idea of the development of reasoning power. Christian teaching recognizes that intellectual ability is one of man's crowning glories, and would encourage us to develop it for the glory of God. But at the same time the Bible warns us that cleverness is not necessary to salvation, and that man's mind has its limitations. We are told that man's evil heart and crooked desires will tend to twist his thinking and produce false judgments. So, while we must encourage our young people to develop their reasoning power, we should also help them to see that to make reason a god is to worship what is imperfect and fallible.

Next, there is the idea of independence in thought and action. The HMSO report already quoted speaks of 'a *proper* sense of independence', and this is a necessary qualification. For all people are ultimately dependent on their Creator: 'In him we live and move and have our being'. The Christian would define a proper independence as a freedom of mind under God. Independence implies to most people a power to choose and make judgments on their own account; but to Christians it implies also a responsibility we have towards God to choose and make judgments according to what we know of his character and purposes. In any case, whatever one's religion or lack of it, independence has to be qualified by the appropriate recognition of social obligations.

Allied to the development of reasoning power and the proper use of this power, is the question of the child's other gifts and abilities, whatever these may be. We wish our children to improve all their talents. Here we should perhaps pause to consider two aspects of talent. To speak in terms of gifts is not to suggest that each child's intelligence and talents are deposited in him at birth in fixed quantities and watertight compartments. They may often come to light as a product of social interaction, of the child's linguistic or emotional development, and of the general education he receives. Skills and aptitudes are certainly discovered – for practical purposes 'acquired' – and developed by such influences. However, it seems clear, both on Scriptural and empirical grounds, that there are inherited differences to distinguish one child's potential and learning from another's. If we aim at the maturity of each individual, we must encourage each person to develop his talents effectively, whether they are innate or acquired, and whether they are academic or practical. We must remember, too, that the most intelligent pupils are not necessarily the most important or worthwhile members of a school community. Christian teaching stresses the value of each person for what he is, not merely for any ability to learn readily or to succeed in examinations.

A second suggestion which Professor Lester Smith mentions as an educational aim is that of character formation. Attitudes on this subject, plus their outworking in practice depend mainly on one's view of the nature of man. Much educational theory begins with man as he is, accepting his 'natural' behaviour as right. The man who has had perhaps the greatest influence in popularizing this view among educationists has been Jean Jacques Rousseau. He rejected the Christian doctrine of original sin, and urged that 'the first impulses of nature are always right'.[9] He certainly deserves the title of 'the emancipator of children' as far as Western education is concerned, for he drew attention to many aspects of childhood unacknowledged in his day but which we now take for granted. 'Nature wants children to be children before they become men' is one of his memorable sayings. His character Julie[10] reminded the educationists of his time and since that 'childhood has ways of seeing, thinking and feeling peculiar to itself'. There was also Pestalozzi, who was an enthusiastic champion of many of Rousseau's views on the nature and education of children and who asserted that 'all instruction of man is then only the art of helping Nature to develop in her own way'.[11]

Such views have been widely accepted in education since they were first propounded by these two men. This line of thinking has been central in this century for example, in the approach of the exponents of the Dalton plan and the more recent advocates of project and discovery methods in teaching. Nature's methods, given guidance, have been found to work, and children as well as teachers have benefited greatly. Education at all levels has become less authoritarian and more child-centred, more 'pupil-related', as *The Fourth 'R'*, the Durham Report on religious education prefers to express it. The teaching profession now acknowledges that a more individual approach to each child is essential if we are to help every pupil to realize his or her full potential as a human being. It does not follow, however, that every child is getting this personal attention in our schools. Too many classes are still far too large. Too many lessons suffer from the lack of up-to-date books and equipment. In many schools it is still not possible for teachers to employ the most appropriate teaching methods or to provide the most suitable educational environment for their pupils. Yet even if we could provide the best methods of teaching in each situation and ideal educational and social surroundings, we could not guarantee that our pupils would grow into mature and fulfilled individuals, although with these advantages this result should be the logical outcome of Rousseau's view that 'the first impulses of nature are right'.

However, as has been already stated, new child-centred teaching methods are not without their good effects, and Christians would agree that we should continue to improve as best we can all aspects of the education service. Every child is precious to God, and therefore we have a responsibility towards each child to help it to grow in character as God intends. This also means, as the Newsom Report reminds us,[12] that our responsibility is as much towards the 'C' and 'D' stream pupils as towards those of better intellectual ability. We should ensure that 'the rejected', as David Holbrook has called them,[13] receive the constant care and attention they need. At the moment they cannot all receive such attention, for buildings and equipment are often inadequate, and undue stress is often laid upon academic qualifications and training. Too many handicapped and below-average pupils have to make their way alongside their more fortunate contemporaries in environments wholly unsuited to their needs. Christians should be concerned about such circumstances, and indeed should strive to maintain the personal touch in school life at all points, for we are concerned with people as individuals. It is when teachers and pupils really know one another personally that educational aims will most probably be realized. And only with such shared knowledge and understanding does the school become a meaningful reality.

'Education is not a process of packing articles in a trunk', said Whitehead,[14] who believed that the purpose of education was 'to stimulate and guide self-development'.[15] Clearly we want to encourage the rich diversity of human life and character in man. We wish to foster qualities of independence, self-reliance and assurance, and the ability of all pupils to help themselves wherever possible. As has already been hinted, Christian teaching sounds a warning note here. Because children are not born 'naturally good', because all human beings are fallible creatures, teachers and pupils need to recognize that self-development should not become an end in itself and that self-reliance should have limitations. We all need to acknowledge our dependence in so many spheres on one another, on those who are older or more experienced, and above all on God himself. In the world of school the children can be helped to understand what this dependence involves and can have the Christian point of view explained.

Friedrich Froebel, a keen advocate of free activity methods in the upbringing of children, rightly stressed that education 'should lead and guide man to clearness concerning himself and in himself'.[16] He said that the object of education is 'the realization of a faithful, pure, inviolate, and hence holy life'.[17] But he recognized that a right relationship with God is essential if an individual is to achieve such a result. Most educationists hope that their teaching will help to produce 'good', or 'better' men and women. Christians differ from others in their definitions of these terms. Their standpoint is governed by their understanding of the nature of man, and also of God, as revealed in the person and life of Christ. Christian teaching indicates that because of the marring effects on human nature of what the Bible calls 'sin', all educational effort has serious limitations as regards the making of 'good' people. While education can help the young to understand much about right and wrong, and what is good or bad in different spheres, it cannot *empower* them always to want or choose the best. Nor is the removal of sin and its effect an aim or task of education. Not just Christians, but all sensible people recognize the peculiarly human character of man, in that his reach exceeds his grasp. He is always falling short of his own aspirations.

The main content of Christian teaching is sometimes summed

up as 'the law' and 'the gospel'. There is no contradiction between the two, as some writers have declared. They are essential to each other. It is not the duty of Christian educationists to preach the gospel in their lessons, but most Christians think it vital to help children to know about and understand the teaching of the Old and New Testaments. Such teaching is especially relevant concerning the formation of character. It presents a standard at which the pupils can aim. It can aid them, through its frank descriptions of human nature and its many variegated character studies, to arrive at an understanding of self, so basic to personality development. It also assists children in understanding others and in forming relationships. Lastly, if taught clearly and sympathetically, it encourages good behaviour and wholesome social living, by helping to promote outward conformity to its maxims through the learning of self control. Character development is the most crucial aspect of the work of parents and teachers. Most Christians believe that Biblical teaching provides them with realistic, practical help to enable them to base their instruction rightly. It is – both for those who learn and for those who teach – a lamp to make clear where one stands, and a light to indicate the way forward.

The third objective Professor Lester Smith refers to is equipment to earn one's living. Vocational guidance is an important part of schooling. Teachers want to help their pupils at least to lay the foundations of future occupational effectiveness. There are excellent special courses in many secondary schools which prepare the way directly for the professional training and experience children will have when they begin to earn their living. Direct vocational training ought to be limited in school, however, since to over-emphasize such work might restrict the all-round education that each child needs. Of course some of the general requirements people need when they start work already form part of the curriculum in schools – the use of language, basic handicrafts, mathematics and aspects of citizenship, for example. Most schools try to help their pupils to foster talents which may be of use in their future vocations. Also through talks, films, counselling, discussion and visits, it is possible to help children to discover and fulfil responsible roles.

If children have to earn their living when they leave school, they also have to take their part in other ways in the adult world. Official reports on education have usually stressed somewhere the need to equip pupils to 'play their part in the world'.[18] The first suggestion which the Plowden Report makes in its chapter on educational aims is 'to fit children for the society in which they will grow up'.[19] The report modifies the starkness of this first statement, however, by adding soon afterwards that 'children need to be adaptable and capable of adjusting to their changing environment'. Most parents and teachers, whether Christian or not, probably have these ideas in the back of their minds. They hope that their children will always behave responsibly at home, at work, and as citizens in society. They want them to establish and maintain wholesome relationships with others. They would support St Paul's advice to the Corinthians: 'Do not be children in your thinking; be babes in evil, but in thinking be mature.'

This is right and proper. But let us see where this idea of fitting a child for the society in which it will grow up can lead if we are not careful. Thirty years ago the Spens Report wished children to 'grow up in conformity with the national ethos'.[20] More familiar slogans since the second world war have been: 'we must educate for society', and 'education for democracy'. None of these expressions is in harmony with Christian purposes for education. Christians acknowledge the duty of rendering to Caesar (society, the state, the government) the things that are Caesar's, but do not acknowledge Caesar as having absolute rights over the whole person. If the ends of education are becoming political and social, Christians have the right and duty to object. Naturally, the claims of the society in which one lives cannot be ignored by its education service. The community rightly expects its children to be taught responsible behaviour and attitudes, and rightly demands of all its members proper and considerate conduct in their living. The Christian should automatically strive to be a good citizen. Nevertheless 'the welfare of society', or 'the good of the state', or 'the needs of the community' (whatever these phrases may mean) are not claims which over-ride all others. If we view the individual as always subservient to the requirements of the state, we deny the Christian view of man. The state is made up of individuals, and the Bible teaches that both the individual and the state are accountable to God for the way they discharge their responsibilities.

An even more common slogan is that education should fit man for his environment. General though this statement is, one can read into it much that commands wide approval. We do have to prepare our children to face the world in which they live, taking particular account of local and national conditions. We need to help them to adapt themselves to much that will be demanded of them in their social and working lives. But Christianity underlines that man is the supreme creation of God. To set up his environment, therefore, as the *determining* standard for his education is to try to reverse Christian values. It is also a very static policy. Social and economic needs are important. Good citizenship matters. Each person should be 'subject to the governing authorities' since they are 'instituted by God', and he should render to every man his due.[21] Yet if the social purposes of education are to subordinate the needs of the individual to those of the state, then the balance which the Bible commends is lost.

One of the Bible's chief concerns is to promote balanced living. It stresses that man is concerned both with the natural world and with his fellow men. That it can enlighten even very young minds in this respect can be illustrated from the answer of a seven-year-old Stockton child to questions on the Garden of Eden before the Fall. He wrote: 'The Garden of Eden was a happy place because it was full of fruit and vegetables and because nobody was lonely there.' The rest of the class voted this the best answer of all. It certainly illustrates something of the truth that Christian living includes the wholehearted enjoyment of material things balanced by a recognition that personal relations are supremely important. Teaching children about their responsibility towards the natural world would include encouraging them in the right use of its resources, and in this also Christians have a responsibility.

Professor Lester Smith mentioned a fourth widely held educational aim. He described this as 'the transmission and improvement of the cultural heritage'. Most Christians would give qualified approval to this goal. Each generation inherits so much from its past that is worth trying to understand, and there is so much to enjoy. Every new period in turn may well have much that is worth maintaining or developing for future advantage. The study of the good, the beautiful and the true is always very satisfying. Everyone should be able to enjoy as much as they can of these things. We want our children's lives to be richly furnished. For they need to pass on a worthwhile inheritance to their children. This cultural heritage is not limited to the treasures of created beauty of various kinds. It includes society and its institutions. We must help our pupils, therefore, to understand the customs and organization of their country and of their immediate social community.

Paul, speaking to the men of Athens, reminded them that God 'made from one every nation of men to live on all the face of the earth, having determined allotted periods and the boundaries of their habitation, that they should seek God, in the hope that they might feel after him and find him'. Each nation has its own language, traditions and national culture. Christians believe that every good endowment and every perfect gift is God-given and that he wants us to enjoy them. Paul again, writing to the Philippians urges them to think about the good, pure, true, lovely, gracious, excellent and praiseworthy. Men have been liberally endowed with many great gifts, and life can be much enriched through the enjoyment of good literature, music, architecture and the creative arts. Christian teaching implies that education involves more than knowing the best that is known and thought in the world: it involves also making a right use of it and knowing its limitations. Most teachers, whatever their beliefs, will readily help their pupils where they can to enjoy the varied riches of creation, and to develop discernment and better understanding. A specifically Christian contribution would be also to encourage thankfulness at all times for such benefits.

However, not all that comes down to us from our past is worth passing on. No one wants to pass on things that are evil, or of very dubious value. There are vital problems of selection and censorship in the teaching of children and young people. The particular stage of development through which a group may be passing is not the only determinant governing a teacher's choice of material. The Christian can hardly be expected to encourage his pupils to accept standards or goals which are sub-Christian or anti-Christian. But this does not mean that he should never examine them in his lessons. Ruth Etchells has formulated a useful principle applicable more widely than in the teaching of literature about which she is writing. She points out that 'the Christian view of life being one of wholeness, nothing is too deep for it to contain, too dark for it to counter, too high for it to rise to'. Therefore she suggests that 'there is no writing *fundamentally true of human experience*, which the Christian need fear to read or, at the appropriate moment, share'.[22] While it is not a Christian aim to try to form character solely by reference to a particular cultural pattern, or to fit persons into that pattern, it is right to transmit what is worthwhile, and to endeavour to improve existing cultural standards and activities.

Developing cultural standards, intelligence, character, and a national ethos, and promoting social welfare – these, then, are some of the aims of education. They are all high-sounding aspirations and we have tried to show that it is important to decide what they mean, and how such hopes may be realized in practice. We have seen also that in any case, Christian teaching emphasizes that none of these aims really touches upon man's principal need. The Plowden Report is probably right in asserting that 'general statements of aims . . . tend to be little more than expressions of benevolent aspiration which may provide a rough guide to the general climate of a school, but which may have a rather tenuous relationship to the educational practices that actually go on there'.[23] Nevertheless they do have a definite if limited value in indicating what people regard as of most importance in the educational process.

Is there a delineation of purpose which is characteristically Christian? Most Christians would probably agree that education should make a major contribution to the development of integrated personalities, men and women of God who are thoroughly prepared and equipped for every kind of good work. Some people might argue that the phrase 'of God' adds nothing to the characterization of the aim – if it were omitted, the proposition would be acceptable to Christians and non-Christians alike. But the phrase is necessary for several reasons. It draws attention to the real nature of man, to his origin and to the true purpose of his existence as described in the Bible. Therefore it helps to safeguard the meaning of 'integrated personalities' – balanced, wholesome people like Joshua, Daniel, the Shunammite woman, Paul, Barnabas, Tabitha and countless others, famous and unsung, who in Bible times and since, have shown in their lives the outworking of the grace of God. The phrase is there also to insist on a distinctively Christian element and attitude in the whole educational process. Finally its presence should help to prevent the business of education from becoming completely secular.

All these reasons demonstrate the importance of examining educational aims from a Christian standpoint. The Christian vision of the good life is the highest and most satisfying known to man, just as the Christian view of man is the most realistic and practical there is. It is therefore essential that Christians should test current ideas about purpose in education against the relevant Biblical principles concerning man and his life on earth. By emphasizing the worth, and safeguarding the rights, of every individual, and by pointing the way to balanced, wholesome living, Christian teaching can help to maintain the best standards in our educational theory and practice. Our young people may then be enabled better to understand themselves and to enjoy the riches of creation, whether or not they become Christians themselves.

REFERENCES TO CHAPTER THREE

1 R. S. Peters, *Authority, Responsibility and Education*, Allen & Unwin, 1959, p. 90.
2 *Ibid.*, p. 92.
3 *Ibid.*, p. 92.
4 J. Dewey, *Democracy and Education*, Macmillan, 1916, p. 59.
5 C. Jaarsma, *Fundamentals in Christian Education*, Eerdmans, 1953, p. 232.
6 W. O. Lester Smith, *Education: an Introductory Survey*, Penguin Books, 1957, p. 29.
7 A. N. Whitehead, *The Aims of Education and other Essays*, Williams & Norgate, 1929, p. 6.
8 *Primary Education*, HMSO, 1959, p. 78.
9 J. J. Rousseau, *Emile*, J. M. Dent (Everyman edition), p. 56.
10 In *The New Heloise*, quoted in R. L. Archer (ed.), *Rousseau on Education*, Arnold, 1928, p. 28.
11 In *How Gertrude Teaches Her Children*, quoted in L. F. Anderson, *Pestalozzi*, McGraw Hill, 1931, p. 49.
12 *Half Our Future* (The Newsom Report), HMSO, 1963.
13 D. Holbrook, *English for the Rejected*, CUP, 1963.
14 A. N. Whitehead, *op. cit.*, p. 1.
15 *Ibid.*, in the preface to the book.
16 F. Froebel, *The Education of Man* (trans. W. N. Hailmann), Appleton & Co., 1887, p. 5.
17 *Ibid.*, p. 4.
18 *Half Our Future* (The Newsom Report), HMSO, 1963, p. 29.
19 *Children and their Primary Schools* (The Plowden Report), HMSO, 1967, Vol. I, p. 185.
20 *Secondary Education* (The Spens Report), HMSO, 1938, p. 148.
21 Romans 13: 1, 7.
22 R. Etchells, 'Did God Read Shakespeare?', *Spectrum*, Vol. 1, No. 2, January 1969, pp. 58, 59.
23 *Op. cit.*, p. 186.

Chapter Four
EDUCATION AND THE NATURE OF MAN

Behind every educational system, its aims, curricula, teaching methods and organization, lie assumptions about the nature of man and the purpose of life. These ideas are not always articulated or systematized, nor do they often appear to influence the day-to-day business of learning and teaching. Nevertheless, the way we treat our children and how we bring them up is ultimately determined by our beliefs about their nature and needs. Therefore the questions 'What is man?' and 'What is man's destiny?' must be faced by educationists, for their educational policies will be shaped by the answers they provide.

At the present time, in Britain at least, there are basically two main points of view on this subject which demand attention. The first of these, advocated by a very small but very vocal and able group of secular humanists, maintains that man is the measure of all things. He must not appeal to any supposed power or set of standards outside himself, for he is totally responsible for his life and future. His creeds must all rest upon observable facts, empirically grounded. He must never take what is sometimes (misleadingly) called the leap of faith. It is his destiny to direct the evolutionary process. Ideas concerning supernatural or absolute standards must be rejected because they lead to gross superstition and erect formidable barriers against progress. Properly conducted studies of man and the society in which he lives will reveal the main needs and wants of man, and scientific social engineering – or as H. J. Blackham puts it, 'organized enlightenment and organized pressures'[1] – will enable him to achieve what he desires. So men will bring about ever greater happiness and fulfilment for greater numbers of people.

According to some who support these assertions, man is simply a chance collection of 'metabolizing protoplasm'[2], evolved out of 'the vast meaninglessness of the insentient universe'.[3] He has become dominant by the 'blind, opportunistic workings of natural selection'.[4] His duty is 'to try to understand (the evolutionary process) and the mechanisms of its workings, and at the same time direct and steer it in the right direction and along the best possible course'.[5] The instrument which does the directing and steering is man's reason, and right use of reason will enable man to control himself and his world. Blackham states that 'it is reasonable to think that it is not beyond the wit of man to bring about situations and conditions everywhere in which it will be reasonable for men to behave reasonably'.[6] He does not, however, support this statement of faith with factual evidence. Reason is also seen to supply the answers to man's moral problems. According to Morris Ginsberg, 'man is moralized in proportion as he becomes more rational'.[7] Sir Julian Huxley goes further still in envisaging 'the promised land beyond', which we see by using our 'rational, knowledge-based imagination', man's key 'instrument of vision'.[8]

Education plays a crucial role in helping man to progress towards this better life. According to Huxley, 'the evolutionary idea must provide the main unifying approach for a humanist educational system'.[9] Educators should try to provide children 'with more effective systems of canalising their own moral, intellectual and spiritual development'.[10] Two major tasks are firstly 'to hammer out the details of a general curriculum which . . . would reflect the unitary vision provided by modern science and learning',[11] and secondly, to work out 'how the educational system could encourage the growth of integrated personalities, at war neither with themselves nor with society'.[12] It is H. L. Elvin's view that 'we have to educate so that young people will think of man as an evolving species in an environment that he himself is changing and should change only with consciousness of what he does'.[13]

These opinions about man raise problems to which no adequate solutions are offered. For instance, where is the empirically grounded evidence to show that rational man will be more ethical? Certainly Christians and humanists can agree that morality is more rational than immorality. But while intelligence is necessary to moral development, daily experience shows that though we may be able to think rationally, we frequently behave without that respect and consideration for others which are essential characteristics of morally responsible action. Can man achieve rationality by his own unaided efforts? The secular humanist says 'Yes, man can perfect himself'. The Christian says 'No. Men cannot achieve rationality or reach perfection without the help of divine grace.' Where also is the evidence that man will bring about by his own efforts that 'promised land'? If man is merely an accidental agglomeration of atoms, where does reason come from? If there is no reality outside self which corresponds to our thoughts, how can we prove logic to be true according to a materialist world view? What are logical rules? How can we even know they exist? In any case, as Freud and others have shown, man is controlled as much by his instincts as by his reason. Again if, as Huxley says, 'there are no Absolutes of truth or virtue, only possibilities of greater knowledge and fuller perfection',[14] how can anyone know what is the right direction, or the best course? How can we even use the word 'moral'? What could it mean? If no one pattern of living is 'best or comprehensively or exhaustively good',[15] how can man know whether he as an individual or the race as a whole is making 'moral' progress or not? In the secular humanist system, nothing is really *worth* doing unless some arbitrary value is given to 'worth'. Man lives in a universe of death. If this universe did not have an intelligent causation, one cannot logically say that hope exists there.

Yet as the quotations from their arguments imply, these people are genuinely anxious to improve man's life on earth. They really do want to change the world into a better place for everyone. They are concerned about self-fulfilment for the individual, and also for the well-being of society. Now in their scheme of things, if self-interest conflicts with social welfare, who wins? If moral values are all relative, and we have a universe in which words like 'must' and 'ought' are out of place, how do we answer the adolescent's challenge: 'Why should I give up my self-interests for the sake of society or some future generation?' Furthermore, what is 'happiness', and how can it be assessed? Why should it be a goal at which to aim? We may assume, if we will, that everyone wants to be happy, but that does not show us what anyone ought or ought not to do about it.

The second standpoint about man which deserves consideration is the one that looks outside man for answers concerning his nature and destiny. The most comprehensive statement of this position is the Christian one. It is more exalted and at the same time more lowly than the standpoint just considered. The basic Biblical position is that it is not possible to understand man apart from his relationship to God. As G. C. Berkouwer has noted, 'the most striking thing in the Biblical portrayal of man lies in this, that it never asks attention for man in himself, but demands our fullest attention for man in his relation to God'.[16] He also asserts that 'man cannot be known with a true and reliable knowledge if he is abstracted from this relation to God'.[17] It does not follow from this that the Biblical view regards other relationships – with his fellow human beings and with the rest of creation – as insignificant. Just the opposite, in fact. These relationships are important just because of man's relation to God.

In an excellent and comprehensive book on Christian ethics, Otto Piper helpfully explains the different approaches to reality of secular and theological thinking. He points out that 'whereas the secular approach to reality is a bilateral one, that of theology is a triangular relationship. In secular mentality subject and object, man and his partner, individuality and collectivity etc. are supposed to stand on the same level. In the field of knowledge the result is doubt and uncertainty and in the field of action, likewise, one must content oneself with a compromise, all other factors being equal'. He notes the danger of one component factor arbitrarily or with insufficient reason being described as superior, with no way in which the prejudice can be overcome. He then goes on: 'In theological thinking both earthly factors are related to the will of God, with the result that not only each earthly factor but also their mutual relationship are rooted in God's will. Accordingly man does not simply happen to find himself in this world. Rather he has a field of action assigned to him and so a determined sphere of operation. Thus people I meet are my fellow men and neighbours, people entrusted by God to my care.'[18]

Biblical teaching primarily emphasizes the supreme worth and dignity of every human being. Some much-quoted words from the Book of Psalms provide a good illustration of this. In Psalm 8 we read:

'When I consider thy heavens, the work of thy fingers, the
 moon and the stars, which thou hast ordained;
What is man, that thou art mindful of him?
 and the son of man, that thou visitest him?
For thou hast made him a little lower than the angels,
 and hast crowned him with glory and honour.
Thou madest him to have dominion over the works of thy hands;
 thou hast put all things under his feet.'

Man is the creation of God and he is 'fearfully and wonderfully made'. He is a person who enjoys a special relationship with his Maker, who has chosen him to carry out significant tasks in his world. Man is the most excellent example of all the works of God. His capacity for fellowship with God, his beauty, his many wonderful gifts and his potentiality for great good all bear witness to this fact. The reminder in Psalm 49 that man 'is like the beasts that perish' – that man must accept his creatureliness, in humble dependence on his Creator – in no way detracts from his worth or distinctiveness.

Man is the supreme creation, but being a creature he is dependent upon his Maker. 'Apart from me you can do nothing', Christ warned his disciples, and in the New Testament, readers are more than once reminded of his quotation from Deuteronomy 8, that man shall not live by bread alone but by every word of God. He cannot fulfil his destiny or understand the meaning of his life without the strength and the insight which God alone can give him. Man was created to enjoy perfect fellowship with God. His glory and worth are underlined first in the divine nature of his origin, and then confirmed when God in Christ took human form at the incarnation. No other system of thought and belief so fully stresses man's great dignity and value. The most important implications of this for education are that the worth and importance of every single child, however gifted or handicapped, however likeable or irritating, should be clearly acknowledged. All deserve the best that their society can do for them. To discriminate therefore in favour of one particular individual or group at the expense of the rest would be very wrong. Indeed one immediately practical outcome of this teaching for those who accept it, is that it helps them, if they are ever tempted to favour or criticize certain pupils more than their fellows, to deal more justly with all their classes.

It is worth making brief mention of one other point about man's creation. This is that God created man in his own image. The medieval Scholastic view of this was that the image was something added on to human nature and that there was in fact a clear division between the material and the spiritual. Hence the supposed dualism between matter and spirit. One deduction from this belief is that man is not therefore a religious being intrinsically, in very essence. If this were so, then one could speak, for instance, of secular and religious education as though they were two distinct and separate forms of training which cannot and should not be fused.

The Reformers, however, and others since, have said that the image of God is essential to human nature, and that to deny this is to deny that man is truly human. In other words, a description of human nature which makes no reference to man's religious nature, is incomplete. To say that man is rational and moral and to overlook or deny that he is a religious entity is to present only a partial picture. Man is rational and moral *because* he is a religious entity. Also such a division as the Scholastics urged is certainly not known in one's own self-consciousness. Modern psychology generally supports the view that there is a basic unity in human experience. Educational implications again follow from this idea of man as essentially a unity. For instance, an upbringing which concentrates almost entirely upon the development of pupils' cognitive powers is too unbalanced. The 1944 Education Act adopts the right approach in its statement that 'it shall be the duty of the local education authority for every area, so far as their powers extend, to contribute towards the spiritual, moral, mental and physical development of the community by securing that efficient education throughout those stages shall be available to meet the needs of the population of their area'.[19] Such a requirement properly makes explicit the importance of all-round development.

One of the main weaknesses, from the Christian standpoint, of the secular humanist doctrine of man is that its view of man is not sufficiently tragic. The statement by H. J. Blackham about reasonableness, quoted early in this chapter, well illustrates this fact. The doctrine recognizes much that is good in man and acknowledges his great potential for enriching the quality of life. It deplores man's inhumanity to man during his history but fails adequately to explain the evil in man, taking it for granted that man can by his own efforts gradually eradicate all the ills that flesh is heir to. But this attitude is unrealistic and unsupportable. The vision of the wholly reasonable, autonomous man is but a vision, something to aspire to but impossible to attain. The Biblical argument is that man has rebelled against God, trying to change his creatureliness to be like God, because he wants to be the absolute arbiter of his own affairs. This deliberate disobedience to God is called sin. Sin is definite evil, not merely a limitation of man's nature, or simply anti-social behaviour. The New Testament teaches that all men everywhere have sinned. And without the grace of God they will go on sinning. They may set before themselves noble, heart-warming ideals, but the fact of sin means that they will not, indeed cannot by their own efforts, achieve them.

The principal result of this rebellion is guilt before God. A second consequence is moral pollution. The whole of man's personality has been affected and influenced by sin. This does not mean that man is henceforth utterly incapable of anything good and valuable, but that all aspects of his nature are to some extent marred. His thinking, feeling, willing, speaking and acting are all adversely affected. The good that he tries to do, including even his attempts to worship, is tainted and imperfect. He cannot by his own efforts live in a right relationship with God. Hence he is also no longer able to maintain harmonious relationships with all his fellow human beings. That this really is the case can be seen daily in the everyday life of each person. In regarding himself as the arbiter of his fate and able in his own strength to accomplish his own ends, he loses his freedom. What seems an act of liberation – in following the devices and desires of his own heart – in fact enslaves him. Sin exerts a stranglehold which only God can loose. The harder man tries to assert himself and establish his own authority over his life, the more hopelessly bound he becomes.

Man is not the measure of all things, nor is he inherently good. It follows from this that the argument is erroneous which says that man's main task is to provide the right, properly equipped environment to ensure the successful upbringing of our children. We must indeed try to create healthy and attractive surroundings for them at home, at school and in the local neighbourhood, for such a background gives parents, teachers and children alike a better chance to succeed in their educational work. But a satisfying social, cultural and educational setting will not overcome the inherent weaknesses of man's nature.

When we have said all this, human beings are still rational and moral creatures. They still have some ability to distinguish between good and evil. Their problem is not that they are ignorant of what is right but that too often they do not *want* what is right. They still have some appreciation of the good, the beautiful and the true, and some creative ability. They also retain some sense of the divine, as is shown in the general human urge to worship, evidenced in every kind of human society ever known. Furthermore men can, by their own efforts, overcome some of the problems of life, of government, of study, and of relationships with others. Yet sin is deeper than the personality problems that it causes. Its nature and universality mean that only God can deal effectually with it.

In the light of this teaching it is foolish for men to put their faith only in their own reason, and to try to interpret the whole of life solely by reference to themselves. Now it is almost certainly the case that men discover knowledge in science and mathematics by independent reasoning, and there may well be truth in the claim that in the first instance something of man's moral knowledge is similarly acquired. But men cannot through their unaided reason understand and effectively interpret the whole of reality. Some people argue that twentieth-century man is free to do just this, being master of his own destiny. But freedom which ignores God is, as R. J. Rushdoony says, 'merely a desire for self-indulgence and an escape from responsibility'.[20] He also comments that 'the kind of freedom often claimed by modern man is not the freedom of the creature but that of would-be gods'.[21] True freedom, as F. W. Garforth has stated, 'is often proportionate to obedience to law'.[22] Christianity teaches that man is most truly free when he is fulfilling the purpose for which he was created – to obey and glorify God.

The doctrine of man to which we hold fast influences us in many important ways. It affects the standards and values we have and determines in particular our attitudes to other people. It has its effect on the way we behave as individuals and on our conduct generally. If, for instance, we believe that other people just happen to be there to be used in various ways for our own self-fulfilment, then we shall be more concerned about our rights and privileges than about our duties and responsibilities. We may place greater value on independence, contentment, personal stimulation and satisfaction than on respect for others, sympathy, honesty and self-denial. We shall certainly feel that it is more blessed to receive than to give. If, however, we recognize others as God-created like ourselves, we are more likely to treat them with the respect and concern which are their due. Our doctrine of man prescribes the goals which we set for ourselves and our children, and helps us to decide about purpose in life. Do we tell our families that they must get what they can while they can and to stand up for themselves since no one else will do this for them? Or do we urge them to love their neighbour as themselves, as God loves them? Not least, our view of man helps to shape our educational theory and practice.

What are the consequences, for education, of the Scriptural teaching about the nature and destiny of man? Two of the most important have already been mentioned. The first concerns the value of every individual child. No one person in his essential nature is of greater or lesser worth than another. Consequently all children should be helped and encouraged as much as possible throughout their school lives. A system which concentrates on a favoured few or neglects the exceptional in attending to the majority is intolerable. On the other hand, this high view of man does not proclaim that the rights of the individual are always superior to those of society, thus threatening the legitimate authority of the state. A person's true value is seen in his individual personality, and his education at all stages should provide the individual nurture and help he needs. At the same time, in encouraging individual development Christianity does not sanction self-assertion. For it stresses that man has to live in terms of his own nature, and that to do this is to live in terms of God's law.

The second consequence relates to the need to provide for all pupils a balanced, all-round education which concerns itself with the development of the whole child. All needs, spiritual, moral, mental and physical should be catered for. Because it is possible for men to do good and to be creative, a nation's education service should strive to develop individual potential and to help pupils to acquire and develop skills and talents which they can use for their own satisfaction and for the good of their community. For wherever they can help to improve man's life on earth, most people would wish them to try to do so. An all-round education will also involve helping them to come to some understanding of themselves, and of human nature generally. The Bible indicates that they would need to face up to man's limitations as well as his potential. For whether he likes it or not, man is restricted by his own nature, by the presence of others and by the world in which he lives, and he has to face the fact of the presence and the law of God. The total picture is neither over-optimistic, nor unduly pessimistic, but realistic. There are problems about man which he can never solve by himself. He will never succeed in creating utopia because he will never be able to free himself from his sinfulness and its consequences. Yet there is also real hope of success, if he acknowledges his relationship to God. For where man is at his most helpless, God can deliver him and enable him to live in harmony with others and with himself.

The Biblical doctrine of man suggests two other major tasks for educationists. Firstly, children require help to understand the world in which they live, and also the part that man has so far played in the world. One of the first commands which God gave to man, a command that has never been revoked, stated that man was to control and subdue the earth, and have dominion over all living things. It follows that all children need to know as much as they can about both their physical and their social environment, so that they may in due course play their part in making proper and effective use of all the riches of creation. Man must also, as Sir Julian Huxley rightly says, abandon the irresponsible exploitation of the natural world, and learn 'to co-operate and conserve'.[23]

Children should be encouraged to respect the created order and to experience the wonder of its majesty and variety. Studies in the history of science and of man have a valuable contribution to make here too. Perhaps they most of all can alert pupils to the attractions and the challenge of their world. By demonstrating man's past and present successes and failures in coming to terms with his environment, they provide information and guidelines by which each new generation may chart its own course.

The second task is related to the need to provide pupils with a moral and ethical foundation for life in the course of their education. For one thing that ought to come out of the various teaching programmes in all schools is understanding concerning standards and values, those related to everyday life as well as those inherent in the different subject disciplines. Our society readily recognizes the need to teach science, mathematics, languages, social studies and vocational subjects and skills. It is important that our pupils should also experience and ponder on the good, the true and the lovely, especially because of the corrupting effects of sin and evil. Moral education, which includes direct moral teaching, is essential. Children should have the chance to acquire moral knowledge and understanding, and be given opportunities to exercise moral judgment. Their religious education is similarly important. Therefore an adequate time allowance should be given in school for these studies. The absolute standards of truth and goodness about which the Bible teaches provide a framework against which to measure oneself, and direction when one is uncertain or confused. Along with (many would say 'part of') this training in moral and religious awareness is guidance concerning personal and social responsibility. This need is highlighted by the constant emphasis in the Bible that man is a responsible person who is accountable for all that he thinks and says and does. It may be worth adding that, for the good of society, to develop the moral sense of children is more important than the development of intellect, since when a nation's moral sense decays, so also does its social structure. Effective social organization will not guarantee sound morality in a society. But a morally healthy people will almost certainly enjoy purposeful life characterized by stability, order and confidence.

Christian standards and values have helped to form the structure of our society in Britain, and have permeated its thinking for centuries. So it is hardly surprising that many of those who would not profess to be Christians, would nevertheless agree with most of the above comments about the education of our children. This means that, despite differences of faith, Christians and non-Christians can and do collaborate harmoniously in the education service. It does not follow from this, however, that as long as a reasonable measure of agreement can be reached in practice, no one need bother unduly about the underlying theoretical presuppositions. Unless the principles which lie behind and which instigate action are sound and true, such agreement will soon disappear, and we shall lose our way in the dark. We must therefore examine them regularly, and make them explicit. Christians claim that their beliefs are realistic and thoroughly practical, as well as having logical consistency. They argue also that commitment leads to dynamic, purposeful action. By accurately analysing the nature of man, Christianity, in education as in life in general, can effectively meet the true needs of all children, at the same time acting as a preservative of all that is worthwhile both in school and out.

Education is not the source of man's salvation that many have believed it to be. For education, however thorough and enlightened, cannot prevent man from breaking the law of God and of his own nature. It cannot force its pupils to choose the right course and reject the wrong one at every stage. Man, in spite of his education, can and often does violate his rights and duties if he so wishes, and he will sooner or later have to bear the consequences. For man is a sinner. A rightly oriented education will present to children the fact that responsible choices must be made, choices not just about careers but about attitudes to others, about friends, about one's mode of living, and about the beliefs by which one intends to live. It can prepare its pupils to face up to these choices. It can enable them to appreciate something of the consequences which follow choice. It can help to solve difficulties which may hinder clear understanding of the decisions they may have to make. Many people think it should exhort in favour of the right choices. But exhortation, even if one were sure about the correctness of the choice, is not a method which many teachers would commend today. Education cannot force children to choose right, but it can at least show the difference between good and evil and right and wrong, and offer general principles of guidance. It may even provide sanctions which may ensure that many will outwardly conform to what is right and good. Perhaps education has fulfilled its main responsibilities when it has made quite clear to those being educated what *their* responsibilities are as individuals and as members of society. Christians believe that for this to be accomplished realistically, we need to know and to teach the Biblical view of man's nature and needs, for only this fully explains what is the purpose of life for human beings everywhere. Only through the grace of God will men truly fulfil that purpose. Only through the power of God will they consistently choose and act aright.

REFERENCES TO CHAPTER FOUR

[1] H. J. Blackham, 'The Human Programme', in Sir J. Huxley, ed., *The Humanist Frame*, Allen and Unwin, 1961, p. 137.
[2] Sir J. Huxley, *The Humanist Frame*, Allen and Unwin, 1961, p. 19.
[3] *Ibid.*, p. 18.
[4] *Ibid.*, p. 17.
[5] Sir J. Huxley, *Education and the Humanist Revolution*, The Ninth Fawley Foundation Lecture, University of Southampton, 1962, p. 9.
[6] H. J. Blackham, *op. cit.*, p. 141.
[7] M. Ginsberg, 'A Humanist view of Progress', in Sir J. Huxley, ed., *The Humanist Frame*, p. 113.
[8] Sir J. Huxley, *The Humanist Frame*, p. 20.
[9] Sir J. Huxley, *Education and the Humanist Revolution*, p. 14.
[10] *Ibid.*, p. 26.
[11] *Ibid.*, p. 29.
[12] *Ibid.*, pp. 30–31.

[13] H. L. Elvin, 'An Education for Humanity', in Sir J. Huxley, ed., *The Humanist Frame*, p. 275.
[14] Sir J. Huxley, *Education and the Humanist Revolution*, p. 11.
[15] H. J. Blackham, ed., *Objections to Humanism*, Constable, 1963, p. 19.
[16] G. C. Berkouwer, *Man: The Image of God*, Eerdmans, 1962, p. 195.
[17] *Ibid.*, p. 93.
[18] Otto A. Piper, *Christian Ethics*, Nelson, 1970, p. 48.
[19] Education Act, 1944, chapter 31, Part 2, 7.
[20] R. J. Rushdoony, *Intellectual Schizophrenia*, Presbyterian and Reformed Publishing Co., 1961, p. 111.
[21] *Ibid.*, p. 115.
[22] F. W. Garforth, *Education and Social Purpose*, Oldbourne Press, 1962, p. 51.
[23] Sir J. Huxley, *Education and the Humanist Revolution*, p. 9.

Chapter Five

EDUCATION, GRACE AND CULTURAL GIFTS

The Biblical teaching about sin and its warping effects upon the whole nature of man, raises certain questions. Out of the heart of man spring pride, selfishness, lust, envy and all kinds of other evil. How is it that such evil does not appear to have completely free rein? Why is there not chaos everywhere, with the various nations intent upon destroying one another? There is a certain order and beauty in life. The earth is generally very fruitful. Sinful man still retains some knowledge about God, and some ability to discern good from evil. He promotes outward good behaviour. He acknowledges the existence of virtue. Most people appear to lead reasonably honest, virtuous lives, during which they may well do many good things. They have many gifts and abilities which they usually use effectively for themselves and others. People everywhere seem to have some religious aspirations. How is all this so?

The Christian answers this question by drawing attention to the nature of God, and in particular to his grace. The writer of Ecclesiastes pointed out that 'he has made everything beautiful in its time; also he has put eternity into man's mind, yet so that he cannot find out what God has done from the beginning to the end.' Whilst the world lasts, man can count on the natural order continuing – seedtime and harvest, cold and heat, summer and winter, day and night. God's attitude to mankind in general is marked by great patience and mercy. As Paul told the Athenians, God himself 'gives to all men life and breath and everything'. A comment by John Calvin amplifies this statement. He stated that 'no drop will be found either of wisdom or light, or righteousness or power or rectitude, or of genuine truth which does not flow from Him, and of which He is not the cause.'[1] God is the source and fountain of all goodness. Every blessing in the natural world and in man's personal and social life comes from him.

The term which theologians have most frequently used to summarize this aspect of God's nature and activity is known as 'common grace'. It is grace because it is undeserved kindness to sinners, and it is common because not just Christians but all men everywhere enjoy its blessings. It is an ever-present example of divine mercy which all human beings experience in different degrees throughout their lives, whether they are aware of its source or not. This mercy is revealed in two main ways. The first of these is the restraint of sin. According to many Biblical writers, God by his grace limits the activities of the forces of evil and also curbs the full outworking of sin in the life of each individual and of mankind as a whole. In other words, he keeps the earth from becoming a hell. Secondly, man enjoys the grace of God through his bestowal of many varied blessings. These include natural blessings such as rain and sunshine, food and drink, and also social blessings such as order in national life and the promotion of civil righteousness, or, as Charles Hodge remarks, 'all the decorum, order, refinement and virtue existing among men'.[2]

A number of points can be made in describing the purpose of grace. Of these, three are especially relevant when we are thinking about the Bible and education. Firstly, common grace reveals God's care for all men, not only his church. As Isaiah puts it, he is 'the stability of your times'. In the New Testament we are told that 'he made from one every nation of men to live on all the face of the earth, having determined allotted periods and the boundaries of their habitation.' Stability and order among peoples is God's will. All our children need to be made aware of these Christian claims, as they learn to understand and come to terms with their world, for Christians believe that such claims show us the clearest picture of what God wants for man. Our business is living, and through the preservation of order and the restraint of evil God helps us to keep the stage clear for man's living. God's people can witness, preach and do their work in the world, and all men can thus go about their respective occupations, including that of educating their children.

In the second place, the purpose of common grace is to demonstrate the glorious riches of the created order. These riches abound everywhere, in the natural world and in the society of men and women. Through the grace of God, it is possible for man to discover, develop and use the varied resources of creation for his benefit and enjoyment. Children as well as adults can know the thrill of discovery, the pleasures of creativity, and the satisfaction that comes from experiencing beauty of all kinds. Effective education, on which these activities of men are so dependent, is in turn ultimately dependent on God's grace. Thirdly, in an orderly situation, in which civilization and culture can flourish, it is possible for children and young people to grow to maturity. By contrast the retarded development and unbalance in personality which so often characterize the nature of some adolescents unfortunate enough to come from an unstable background is one sad illustration of this truth. If evil is checked and an ordered society having sound moral values is maintained, then man's natural abilities can be allowed to develop and he can enjoy the blessings of life in the world.

There is a fourth point to make concerning the purpose of common grace. In the many varied cultural gifts through which we experience so much beauty and delight; in the deep insights into human nature and the human condition which great literature and art often provide; in the searching after truth and the analysis of life by the great philosophers and mystics of different ages; in the numerous acts of kindness and selflessness, culminating sometimes in self-sacrifice, which men and women down the centuries have performed for their fellows; and above all in the self-giving love which so many people of all races have experienced in friendships, marriage and parenthood – in all these manifold ways throughout history, human beings have been able to glimpse something of what God intended man to be. Jesus Christ in his earthly life showed most comprehensively and unambiguously God's picture of the true man. Yet in all these other illustrations we can faintly discern part at least of the portrait of man as he was meant to be. This is the grace of God at work once more. No tribe or nation has ever been left without the benefit of this grace. No one can complain that they were left in complete ignorance about their origin and their Maker. God never keeps anyone in total darkness about themselves. He enlightens everyone who comes into the world.

If children are to develop properly they require a stable environment characterized by love and consistency. If at home and at school we provide a secure anchorage, we can more effectively encourage them to move from the known to the unknown, to explore their world and test its values, to use their imagination, and to think critically. If their lives are beset by constant change, by irregularity of habits, by uncertainty of treatment, how can they possibly achieve that assurance, resolution and calmness of spirit which are central traits of the mature adult? How can they recognize the value of purposeful, ordered living? How indeed can they learn anything of worth if their homes and classrooms are not structured by love, understanding and discipline? If the environment is positive and challenging, yet full of sympathetic understanding, children are more likely to respond with the trust that is essential to their progress. Where these values of love, order and consistency exist, there is manifested the grace of God; for there the disruptive, splintering effects of evil have been held back. It is true that there are times in the history of individual nations when it seems that 'chaos is come again'. Perhaps when this occurs the world is witnessing the judgment of God upon some of the evil within that nation. For all sin and all evil are under God's condemnation. The wonder is that he always offers man so much time to repent and amend his ways. Nevertheless, where there is stability, where children can grow up rightly, there God's grace is actively present.

In the Bible there are many illustrations of the benefits we receive by the grace of God. 'The Lord is good to all', proclaims the psalmist, 'and his compassion is over all that he has made.' This goodness is seen first of all in that God providentially maintains life and bestows his gifts upon all men alike. The Epistle of James sums all this up in the statement that 'every good endowment and every perfect gift is from above, coming down from the Father of lights'. The created world is good and beautiful to behold, displaying infinite variety, and providing materials in plenty for food, work and leisure. Man enjoys much wisdom and understanding, technical and creative skill. Calvin, who wrote many helpful comments on the subject of God's grace, commented that 'if the Lord has willed that we be helped in physics, dialectics, mathematics, and other like disciplines . . . let us use this assistance'.[3] Human life is also enriched not merely by the experience of prosperity, but through emotional variety, moral awareness, social skills and aesthetic appreciation.

Christian teaching points out that these cultural gifts have definite limitations. It would therefore be foolish to put one's trust solely in such endowments, making their cultivation the ultimate goal of living. They enhance the quality of life of those who enjoy them, but they cannot either so change man's nature as to restore him to his original perfection, or nullify all the effects of sin in his life. They can add lustre to the daily round but, like every human enterprise, they cannot provide men with the ultimate satisfaction for which they yearn. Even so, with many of his gifts, man can make progress by his own efforts in both the personal and the social spheres. Any study of world civilization reveals the splendid achievements of men and women down the years. A further comment of Calvin's is worth quoting. He noted that 'some men excel in keenness; others are superior in judgment; still others have a readier wit to learn this or that art. In this variety God commends His grace to us, lest anyone should claim as his own what flowed from the sheer bounty of God'.[4] 'Whatever good things are in us', he concludes, 'are the fruits of His grace.'[5]

According to the Christian view, therefore, it is possible, through the grace of God, for mankind to live profitably and enjoyably, using, not squandering, the resources of the natural world, and employing, not exploiting, the individual and collective skills of the human race. (It is worth noting that other religions are here at one with Christianity in the rejection of irreverence towards, and exploitation of all creation.) History abundantly shows that a rewarding social life and culture are possible. In addition to the Hebrew-Christian heritage that affects most of us in some way, we can learn from what was good and beautiful in the civilizations of Greece and Rome, and Renaissance and Reformation Europe, to give the most obvious examples.

At this point it will be worth examining the Bible's comments about the state and also glancing briefly at the question of culture, since education is so much influenced by, as well as being an essential part of, a society and its culture.

As we saw in the previous chapter, a fundamental Christian tenet is that God made man to live in fellowship firstly with himself, but also with others. Unfortunately because of sin, fellowship with God is broken, and human relationships are disrupted too. Consequently in society individuals are – to use a favourite modern euphemism – maladjusted, and anti-social behaviour is frequent. One inevitable result of man's deliberate turning away from God and resistance to his grace is a sick society and a sick culture, and of these there have been many examples in mankind's history. Nonetheless God preserves society, by his grace, from complete disintegration. Civilization and order have continued to provide a sphere for the life and witness of the church, and to offer help to the 'maladjusted'. Many Christians would argue that 'culture' exists and persists principally because of the degree of order maintained by God. Because of grace it has been possible to develop and use the manifold resources of creation; in his grace God created the conditions for society, and culture, to flourish. In the words of the Letter to the Hebrews, he upholds the universe by his word of power; in the words of Genesis, while the earth remains, predictable order will be maintained: both are by the providence and grace of God.

Because man is God's creation, the culture of any nation or group is not something neutral. It has ethical and religious connotations, a fact which Christians should emphasize more frequently than they do. It is easy to forget that any culture reflects, and is therefore coloured by, the moral values and the spiritual condition of the society from which it springs. Matthew Arnold saw culture as the pursuit of our total perfection 'by knowing the best that is known and thought in the world'. It involved 'the harmonious expansion of all powers which make the beauty and worth of human nature'.[6] This definition looks rather sweeping, but in fact it tends to limit the meaning of culture to each man's seeking after self-perfection. T. S. Eliot commented that 'the culture of the individual cannot be isolated from that of the group, and that of the group cannot be abstracted from that of the whole society'.[7] Culture includes good taste, social courtesy, the arts, learning and scholarship, the religious life of a people, and as Eliot pointed out, all their other characteristic activities. Culture is in fact the whole pattern of life of a society. Eliot also remarked that 'no culture can appear or develop except in relation to religion'.[8] For, as we have said, man is God's creation.

In the Bible three distinct spheres of authority receive particular attention. They are the family, the church and the state. Concerning the last of these, no detailed blueprint is laid down, but certain general statements are made. As has already been noted, nations have their periods and boundaries determined by God. According to Romans 13, for example, civil government was instituted by God. The sphere of its authority is the nation, its principal concern being for outward order and conduct. Two main reasons for its institution are to restrain evil and reward good. Public order is preserved by punishing evil and promoting good through the maintenance of peace, justice, respect for the rights and property of others, fair dealing and so on. Its task is to encourage its citizens to live responsibly. It is not part of its duty to preach or spread the gospel, but to maintain proper standards and conditions for the earthly good of its members. In such a situation the church is enabled to do its work.

Let us try to see, then, what is the work of the church in the world, as far as living in a society is concerned. There is no specific, detailed teaching in the Bible on *every* aspect of God's creation. One will not find particular instructions concerning politics and economics, for example, or science, or creative artistic work, although all these activities are referred to from time to time. The point the Bible makes is that like everything else they exist and function under the over-all authority of God. This means that they must be seen in proper perspective. Also such activities should be guided by certain fundamental ethical principles, governing values and purposes, such as concern for truth and respect for persons. Because of the problem of sin, man can misuse these good things for merely selfish ends, and even idolize them. However, artistic form, principles in science, laws in economics, rules in hygiene are usually impersonal and of a technical nature. There is no such thing as Christian economics, or Christian science, or Christian sculpture as distinct from any other type. But it is possible and necessary to work out a Christian approach to these matters, an attitude and use based on Christian values and morality. It is particularly important for Christians in teaching to do this, since it is mainly through the schools that our children and young people are introduced to these activities.

It is not part of the Christian's duty, in a world that is passing away, to try to create a specifically Christian society or Christian culture. Nevertheless his aim will be constructive citizenship, trying to help and influence those around him to seek and find what is best for them. For the more closely the life of a nation conforms to the Christian ethic, the better the quality of its daily living. Christians wish to further God's purpose for human society not only by preaching the gospel but also by helping to disclose and display creation's glorious riches. They wish to uphold God's pattern for society, in opposing for instance the confusion of spheres of authority. The church should not try to take over the role of the state, nor should the state usurp the authority of the parents or rob families of their rights.

Christians should use every opportunity that society and its organization offers to do good to their fellow men, by both private and public action. This means trying to help in the progress and development of all fields of activity in which they are competent to work, whilst preserving the right never to give to the state what belongs to God. Teachers might engage when they can in research into their subject or into educational problems. They might take opportunities, through discussion, writing and the training of student teachers, to share with their colleagues their special insights into their work. They might help to inform and enlighten the society in which they live, about educational issues of which everyone should be aware. In using the general knowledge and skills pertaining to a particular sphere of work, the Christian and non-Christian will often speak the same language. It may well be that in some instances the non-Christian is more competent than his Christian colleague. Both these last two points can be illustrated from the field of education. For instance, in discussing methods of teaching their subject, a group of teachers will agree wholeheartedly about a particular approach and the criteria behind it, without any need to refer to the religious beliefs they may or may not hold. And some of the most dedicated and effective members of the profession have not been professing Christians.

The practical relevance to education of these Biblical ideas concerning common grace, the nature of society and man's cultural gifts is fairly obvious. The educational process itself is one of the means of common grace. Through teaching, children can be given a vision of higher things, a desire for what is good and right, a view of man at his best. The skilled, conscientious teacher, whether he realizes it or not, is through the grace of God helping to further God's purpose for men and women, boys and girls. For he is helping the young to try to live informed, responsible, satisfying lives. If man is to be fruitful, to subdue and have dominion, if he is to live effectively in society, and if he is to enjoy the riches of creation as they stem from nature and man himself, then his upbringing should help him to achieve all these things. As far as is possible, children and young people should learn progressively to utilize, as effectively as they can, all the gifts of God, and to continue doing so throughout their lives. They will not do this unaided and without trained guidance. The Christian doctrine of common grace lies behind all educational efforts to improve individual talents and the general culture. It provides a background understanding of the whole of man's situation. It discourages wrongful pride and glorying in man's own accomplishments. It helps to keep man humble as he recognizes his dependence on God and his mercy. It encourages respect for all worthy achievement and re-emphasizes the need to train *every* child.

Christianity has always taught that it is everyone's duty to help to maintain the stability of society. This means upholding all that is right and good in civic and social life generally, trying all the while to raise standards still higher for the benefit of all. It is very important for children to develop a proper respect for authority and good order. They will learn this respect, and understand the value of disciplined behaviour more readily if they see authority properly exercised and order fairly and sympathetically maintained at home and at school. Training in social living and in moral and social awareness is vital also. When young people understand the significance of moral virtues, it becomes easier for teachers to encourage respect for these values. All this will help to promote civil righteousness and restrain evil. But an essential part of the process is the need to teach and uphold the law of God. For as Calvin has pointed out, through this law 'man's life is moulded not only to outward honesty but to inward and spiritual righteousness'.[9]

Since man's wisdom, knowledge, and technical and artistic skills are among the choicest riches of creation, the development of every child's ability and talents is obviously a central task of all teachers. We want to nurture and develop not only their individual understanding and aptitudes but also their powers of appreciation – of skill, judgment, and of work well done in every sphere of life, not just the artistic. We want to provide plentiful opportunities for them to use their talents for the benefit of themselves and their fellows, and also to recognize the moral implications involved in different human activities. Part of the teacher's function here is to pass on those values and skills of society which will be of most help to children as they grow up – values such as self-control, respect for truth, compassion, personal integrity – and skills of communication, judgment, working and playing with others, as well as technical skills and the other aspects of culture and civilization that men have generally deemed worthwhile. The doctrine of common grace encourages high standards in every civilized pursuit, yet discourages the indiscriminate teaching of all aspects of man's cultural activities. Christians might point out that there are secular standards and patterns of social behaviour and art appreciation such as 'live now, pay later', and 'art for art's sake', as well as secular patterns of work and leisure-time activities. Pupils need help to analyse these, particularly in the light of Christian standards, which provide children and young people with an effective measure that they can eventually apply for themselves if they so wish. The Christian faith is particularly helpful in practical ways concerning moral education, and in the application of its ethical principles to conduct in business, to judgment, and to social relations of every kind.

'If we regard the Spirit of truth as the sole fountain of truth', says Calvin, 'we shall neither reject the truth itself, nor despise it wherever it shall appear, unless we wish to dishonour the Spirit of God.'[10] The doctrine of common grace recognizes the worth of effective work and study whether done by Christians or non-Christians. We should all rejoice in the discovery of God's natural laws and in their effective application for man's benefit. The promotion of all worthy forms of social and creative activity enhances the quality of life for everybody. It follows for educationists that they must encourage their pupils to attain the highest standards of which they are capable. Also it is very important that educational administration and teaching methods should assist and not hinder the pupils as they pursue their various programmes. This means that we should try to offer children as wide a variety of courses as is educationally reasonable, and not restrict them to syllabuses which it is administratively convenient to make available. It means that the day-to-day running of a school should be sympathetic and flexible as well as efficient. It means that the presentation of subject-matter should be based on sound aims, and on an up-to-date understanding of how children learn. If we desire pupils to master mathematics or French, for instance, then they must be taught to comprehend as well as to apply the four rules of number, and to speak the language, not simply to analyze it grammatically. And because in most areas of learning children can do much to improve themselves, there should be plentiful opportunities for self-discovery, and for co-operation between individual children, between pupils and teacher, and between people of differing views.

Finally, Christians in education can make one further contribution which cannot always be expected from those who do not share their commitment. This is to express thankfulness for the upholding providence and enabling grace of God, as well as for all the riches of creation. The New Testament repeatedly requests its readers to be 'always and for everything giving thanks in the name of our Lord Jesus Christ to God the Father'. Out of ingratitude to God comes ingratitude to man, that breeding-ground of coldness of heart and indifference to others. A true sense of indebtedness promotes friendly relationships and in one's personal life leads to dependence and humility, and away from that arrogance of knowledge which puffs up. If thankfulness colours the attitude and approach, education becomes much more wholesome for all concerned.

REFERENCES TO CHAPTER FIVE

[1] J. Calvin, *Institutes of the Christian Religion*, ed. J. T. McNeill, SCM Press, 1961, Vol. I, Book I, chapter 2, p. 41.
[2] C. Hodge, *Systematic Theology*, T. Nelson & Sons 1875, Vol. II, p. 671.
[3] J. Calvin, *op. cit.*, Book II, chapter 2, p. 275.
[4] *Ibid.*, p. 276.
[5] *Ibid.*, Book III, chapter 1, p. 541.
[6] Matthew Arnold, *Culture and Anarchy*, CUP, 1948, p. 48.
[7] T. S. Eliot, *Notes Towards the Definition of Culture*, Faber and Faber, 1948, p. 24.
[8] *Ibid.*, p. 27.
[9] J. Calvin, *op. cit.*, Book II, chapter 8, p. 372.
[10] *Ibid.*, Book II, chapter 2, pp. 273–274.

Chapter Six

WISDOM AND KNOWLEDGE

We live in an age that hungers for knowledge. The demand to acquire information and learning is common to every field of study and to people in all walks of life. Not only are vast resources of money and manpower being poured into the search for new knowledge, but almost everybody, it seems, wishes to become knowledgable in one subject or another. In some respects this desire is readily understandable, because as techniques in industry and commerce become more refined so more people require greater skills and specialist qualifications in their daily work. But knowledge also brings prestige and power. The well-informed person is likely to impress and to exert more influence over others than the untrained and the ignorant. Therefore more and more people are looking to the nation's education service to satisfy their needs in this respect. By improving their education they feel they are bettering themselves and not merely their chances of earning a better living. As a middle-aged lady living in the Midlands who recently gained a university degree argued: 'It's a way to become a somebody, and not be a nobody all one's life.'

There is a good deal of truth in this point of view. But sometimes people confuse knowledge with wisdom. They seem to assume that the more information they or their children acquire, the wiser they will be. They appear to believe that education automatically brings wisdom as well as learning and 'know-how'. This is one reason for the increased pressure many parents exert upon their children to stay on at school or college for as long as possible. Such pressure, generally speaking, is supported by the whole teaching profession, though not for this reason. Biblical teaching also encourages the pursuit of learning. It does not, as is sometimes believed, regard earthly wisdom as of little account. It is a fact that Christians have always been enthusiastically involved in all aspects of education. Yet in the history of the Christian church there have been some who have argued that Christians should not spend concentrated time and effort upon the study of the learning and wisdom of this world. Even today one occasionally meets young Christian students who are somewhat apologetic about the fact that their field of study is French literature or economics – rather than theology, presumably. Now not only does such an attitude clash with the doctrine of common grace discussed in chapter five, it in no way accords with the specific teaching of the Bible on the subject of wisdom and knowledge.

In considering the Christian approach to education, this teaching should not be overlooked. Some brief reference will therefore be made to it now. But at the outset an attempt must be made to define terms, if we are to avoid the confusion mentioned above. Take 'wisdom' first. The Oxford dictionary suggests that it is the power of applying critically or practically the experience and knowledge that one possesses. It is the ability to make a right use of knowledge, to work out a right course of action leading to a desired end. It is the art of making sound judgments. At the practical level, the wise man will be one who can decide the best outcome of a given situation, and also the best way of achieving it. Another definition sees wisdom as the heritage of distilled knowledge and experience of a person or a people. In general, wisdom seems to be a particular excellence of mind revealed in the making of practical and moral judgments.

One cannot conclude from this that only the very learned amongst men possess wisdom. It is not an attribute confined solely to those who have enjoyed long and specialized academic training. There are sages in every walk of life. Appropriate knowledge and experience are indispensable for wisdom, but wisdom is not determined by the amount of knowledge one may possess. The fact that a person has amassed great knowledge and is very erudite does not mean that he is necessarily wise. The art of making judgments is something over and above all the relevant information and experience. Also this information and experience need not be consciously formulated nor need it have been acquired by any formal teaching. Many an uneducated man has shown himself wiser than his well-taught contemporaries. Even so, this is not to decry the acquisition of knowledge. Wisdom is enriched by the knowledge one possesses, though not determined by it.

'Knowledge' is information or practical skill, the theoretical or practical understanding of a topic, or the sum of what is known. It is a person's range of information. The objects of knowledge differ. There is knowledge of cricket, or mathematics, or history, or of a person. There is knowledge *of* and knowledge *about*. As the school child quickly learns, there are different areas of knowledge, each one having its own conceptual scheme. Questions asked in mathematics and physics differ from those raised in the study of history and literature, and the tests for true and false are also different. Perhaps the chief distinction between wisdom and knowledge is that knowledge is made up of the facts, principles and practical experience involved in understanding, and wisdom is seen in the conclusions drawn from what is known. Knowledge informs. Wisdom gives direction.

Biblical authors speak of two kinds of wisdom and two kinds of knowledge. There is earthly wisdom, those acquired insights which bestow the power to make practical applications of one's skill and judgment. This kind of wisdom can belong to good and capable men and women whether they are religious or not. Then there is spiritual wisdom. This is insight that is never acquired but is *given* by revelation, spiritual illumination that comes so often through religious experience. It is wisdom which belongs principally to religious people, men and women whose lives are characterized by reverence for the Lord. A similar distinction can be made about the two kinds of knowledge referred to in the Bible. Knowledge may be acquired, particularly through the senses and through objective study and analysis. This knowledge is available to everybody, in accordance with their intellectual gifts. By contrast there is the knowledge that comes only through mutual commitment in personal relationships. Such knowledge is *given*, or one cannot know at all. The most obvious Scriptural illustration of both kinds of knowledge concerns Jesus Christ. The records of his life, words, deeds, and of his effect on others, provide much material for objective study which will yield a great deal of knowledge *about him*. But the heart of the Christian faith and life is not to know about Christ but to know him personally, as we know our parents, children and friends personally. This knowledge is given only through personal commitment to Christ.

In the Bible, wisdom is something extremely practical, not theoretical. It is concerned with the making of judgments which will affect everything one does in life. It involves assessing all the details relevant to a course of action, and then acting, for the right reason, according to right judgment, and for the right end. Perhaps the chief characteristic of the truly 'wise' man is the inner strength of a quiet mind which expresses itself in self-controlled, balanced, disciplined living. Never wise in his own eyes, such a man stores up knowledge, seeks to increase his understanding, listens to advice and delights in the pure and true. By contrast, folly is always associated with the rejection of wise counsel, with loose living, slothfulness, and wickedness. Its way is always the path of restlessness, discontent and ultimate destruction.

God himself alone is wise in the fullest sense. He knows all things in all realms of life and he also brings to pass what he has determined. Through his creative wisdom he brought into being the universe and man, and he governs the course of history. Man is able to understand something of God's wisdom only through God's gracious revelation of those aspects of himself and his truth which he desires man to know. Of Biblical wisdom, the *New*

Bible Dictionary says: 'Stemming from the fear of the Lord, it branches out to touch all of life. . . . Wisdom takes insights gleaned from the knowledge of God's ways and applies them in the daily walk. This combination of insight and obedience (and all insight must issue in obedience) relates wisdom to the prophetic emphasis on knowledge (*i.e.*, the cordial love and obedience) of God.'[1]

The subject of godly wisdom is a profound study requiring far more detailed treatment than is possible here. However, at the risk of superficiality, a number of points are worth listing. Wisdom is one of the attributes of God. Job declares: 'With God are wisdom and might; he has counsel and understanding.' 'He is wonderful in counsel, and excellent in wisdom', says Isaiah. 'He reveals deep and mysterious things; he knows what is in the darkness, and the light dwells with him', adds Daniel. James in the New Testament describes it this way: 'The wisdom from above is first pure, then peaceable, gentle, open to reason, full of mercy and good fruits, without uncertainty and insincerity'. Such is the tenor of both the Old and the New Testaments on the subject. God's wisdom is infinitely superior to man's wisdom. His thoughts are higher than ours and his understanding is unsearchable. His wisdom has inexhaustible depths and riches. But, as Professor C. K. Barrett has pointed out in examining the Biblical background of John's *logos* doctrine, by the time we reach the Book of Proverbs, wisdom is revealed to be more than just an attribute of God. He notes that 'already in Proverbs, the Wisdom of God has ceased to be merely the quality of being wise; Wisdom has an independent existence in the presence of God, and also bears some relation to the created world. . . . Wisdom becomes, more and more, a personal being standing by the side of God over against, but not unconcerned with, the created world'.[2]

Wisdom is seen in all the works of God. It was manifest in the act of creation and may be detected in the beauty, order and variety still to be seen in the created world. It is further revealed in all God's providential dealings and in his rule of man, through the law, through the control of sin – preventing its complete destruction of mankind – and through the work of salvation, redemption and sanctification. If man is to know anything of God's wisdom, he is utterly dependent on revelation by the Holy Spirit. Both Solomon, in his prayer recorded in the first chapter of 2 Chronicles, and Paul, in 1 Corinthians 2, underline this very strongly. For no one comprehends the thoughts of God except the Spirit of God. As Paul commented, what he taught others of the 'secret and hidden wisdom of God' was not taught him by human wisdom but taught by the Spirit, interpreting spiritual truths to those who possess the Spirit (and who can therefore receive and understand them). Finally – a point which links up strongly with Professor Barrett's reference to Wisdom in the Book of Proverbs – Christ is the embodiment of both the power of God and the wisdom of God. Christians are taught that Christ himself is their wisdom, as he is their righteousness, sanctification and redemption. For they have 'the mind of Christ', and in him are all the treasures of wisdom and knowledge.

Concerning human wisdom, the *New Bible Dictionary* makes another useful comment. 'Even wisdom derived from natural abilities or distilled from experience is a generous gift, because God's creative activity makes such wisdom possible'.[3] Nowhere in Scripture is such wisdom and its benefits, and the knowledge on which it rests, disparaged. A helpful statement on this matter comes in Calvin's commentary on the words in 1 Corinthians 1: 20, where the question is asked: 'Has not God made foolish the wisdom of this world?' He wrote: 'By wisdom, Paul here means whatever man can comprehend not only by his own natural ability but also by the help of experience, scholarship, and knowledge of the arts. . . . For what is more noble than the reason of man, by which he stands out far above all other creatures? How greatly deserving of honour are the liberal sciences, which refine man in such a way as to make him truly human! Besides, what a great number of rare products they yield. Who would not use the highest praise to extol statesmanship, by which states, empires and kingdoms are maintained? – to say nothing of other things! ... Paul does not entirely condemn either the natural insight of man, or wisdom gained by practical experience, or education of the mind through learning, but what he affirms is that all those things are useless for obtaining spiritual wisdom.'[4]

These remarks fairly summarize the Christian attitude to the wisdom of this world, and correct the misinterpretations sometimes made not only of the particular passage in 1 Corinthians but of the whole Biblical attitude to human wisdom. Man's understanding and insight have definite limitations, nor will he ever be able to know all things for himself by his own efforts. The wisdom of this world suffers the great handicap of lacking in itself the insight which revelation gives. It has to found itself therefore on its own shared intuitions and collective experience. This means in effect that when faced with the deepest basic problems of human existence, unaided wordly wisdom falls down. It can make valiant attempts to grapple with these difficulties, but needs the light of revelation and the way of the cross to achieve success. Man may possess great natural gifts, but he cannot by these either come to a true knowledge of God, or save himself from his human predicament. Man may be capable of great intellectual perception, as modern scientific discovery and Greek philosophy illustrate, but, as Charles Hodge once said, 'Whatever its value in its own sphere and for its own ends, philosophy cannot save man.'[5] Earthly wisdom is not therefore useless, and to be spurned. It has its honoured place in the scheme of things. But the danger is that men will idolize it, and expect it to provide answers where it is not competent to help. Just as the use of scientific method is the way to progress in understanding the natural world, whereas it is irrelevant and useless in solving problems of moral behaviour, so the wisdom of this world is of great help in understanding the things of this world, but of no avail in helping us to know God. What Scripture condemns is man's tendency to overlook the limitations of natural wisdom and natural knowledge, and set up speculative systems of belief as providing knowledge of

God. For the limitation of earthly wisdom is that 'the world did not know God through wisdom'.

Spiritual knowledge is basically concerned with an individual's personal knowledge of God, knowledge which comes through trust and obedience. Perhaps the most striking Scriptural references to earthly knowledge are in connection with particular individuals. Moses, Daniel and his three friends, Solomon – who apparently possessed great knowledge in the natural sciences – and Paul are outstanding examples. All were well-educated and extremely able men of considerable learning. This they used, along with their spiritual insight, in their day-to-day affairs. The Book of Proverbs encourages all its readers to seek out knowledge and understanding wherever they can. The New Testament has certain reservations about knowledge which qualify this injunction. It reminds us that all man's knowledge is inevitably incomplete and imperfect in this life. Also, knowledge does not last for ever – it will pass away. And knowledge by itself puffs up and makes vain. All these points are a warning to men not to place too much trust in the knowledge they have or are acquiring. It is not an end in itself.

All this has clear implications for the classroom. Acquired 'natural' knowledge and wisdom are of inestimable value. They have obvious practical applications in everyday life. A sound academic content should characterize all school timetables. Presentation of knowledge should be ordered and systematic, using all the modern techniques of teaching. We need to initiate all our pupils into all the main ways of acquiring truth. Allowing them to wander at will through an undifferentiated maze which we may call the humanities, or general studies, or the integrated day is not good enough. For what they know helps to shape what they are and will become as persons. Therefore they must be given some grasp of every distinct field of knowledge. *How* they acquire and master knowledge also influences the way they develop. As well as learning the different methods and techniques of obtaining information and skills, pupils need to recognize the demands of patience, diligence, integrity, openness and a real concern for truth which are made upon all who undertake serious study. They have to learn to have a proper reverence for all data, and how to submit themselves to the evidence available.

The extent to which children gain knowledge and skills depends on their individual ability and the way they are taught. Teachers must obviously select their material and use methods appropriate to each stage of their pupils' growth and ability. It is not difficult to impart knowledge. The great problem for every teacher is how to ensure that each child will make this knowledge a part of himself, and how to help each pupil to use that knowledge to acquire wisdom. Teaching techniques will depend on many variables – the nature and needs of each individual child, his age, intellectual ability, background, previous experience, the skill and personality of the teacher, and so on. One effective way to help children to master their material and achieve insight and sound judgment concerning its application is through project and other work which involves pupils in using what they know and discovering more for themselves. We need to extend their personal experience as widely as possible, since wisdom arises out of both knowledge and experience. An unchanging diet of predigested, third- and fourth-hand information is not adequate at all. Even so, heuristic methods are not a complete recipe for learning. Many a child will seek and seek and never find unless he is helped. And if we take the view that our pupils will discover Shakespeare or Beethoven or even moral rules when they need to, then some of them if left to themselves are going to go through life aesthetically and morally impoverished.

As the Bible reminds us, children need also to recognize that earthly knowledge and wisdom have definite limitations. Learning and technology are not to be made into gods to be worshipped. All pupils must be informed about spiritual wisdom and knowledge. Such information will underline for them the supreme importance of personal relationships, which in a busy world of getting and spending can so easily be neglected. They will need help to understand that these treasures are given, and cannot be obtained through the wisdom and knowledge of this world. It is particularly important in this technological age for young people to realize that human techniques of acquiring knowledge, particularly the methods of science, are appropriate only for those areas for which they are designed. Objective observation, experiment and inductive reasoning are excellent tools for the study of the natural world and the way it works. They are of little or no use to gain the knowledge which only comes through personal involvement and commitment – as in aesthetic appreciation, religious experience, and making friends. If you wish to go through a door, you must have the right key. What is more, pupils must recognize that a sense of proportion is vital in any person's approach to learning.

One result of all this teaching should be that each child will be equipped to act more effectively both as an individual and in co-operation with others. Consequently, under God, the advantages of common grace to mankind in learning, wisdom and practical skill will continue for the following generations. Furthermore, every pupil can be given a fuller understanding of himself and his fellows, recognizing and learning to value their abilities as well as his own. If Biblical teaching is heeded, he will learn that the more true wisdom a man has, the less arrogant, more humble he will be. Here again the Christian approach to wisdom and knowledge shows its worth. It enables us to see these treasures in proper proportion and with humility. It therefore provides a strong curb to man's pride and to his temptation to idolize wisdom and learning. For these are not the only, nor are they necessarily the greatest, of human virtues and achievements. The ignorant and the unwise are not to be despised, nor should they be regarded as second-class citizens. We all – adults and children alike – ought to keep in mind that the final test of true wisdom and of that supreme knowledge which man can know through the gift of God – the knowledge of God himself – is our obedience to the law of God. This compliance reveals itself in righteous living and conversation, and in a practical concern for one's fellow men.

REFERENCES TO CHAPTER SIX

[1] *New Bible Dictionary*, Inter-Varsity Fellowship, 1962, art. 'Wisdom', p. 1333.
[2] C. K. Barrett, *The Gospel According to St. John*, SPCK, 1955, p. 128.
[3] *New Bible Dictionary*, p. 1334.
[4] J. Calvin, *The First Epistle of Paul to the Corinthians*, trans. J. W. Fraser, Oliver and Boyd, 1960, p. 38.
[5] C. Hodge, *Systematic Theology*, T. Nelson and Sons, 1875, Vol. II, p. 102.

Chapter Seven

CHILDREN AND PARENTS

One aspect of Biblical teaching most obviously relevant to education is that concerning children and parents. This teaching is scattered throughout the Old and New Testaments. It looks at the nature, needs, duties and privileges of the young, and gives precise directions to parents and others responsible for the care and upbringing of children. The instruction is detailed, practical and delivered with urgent insistence. It is the purpose of this chapter simply to gather together and present this clear and down-to-earth teaching in a systematic form.

Earlier in the book it was mentioned that in the Bible attention is drawn to three main spheres of authority in human life. These are the family, the church and the state. The vital importance of the family is emphasized in Scripture from the first, one main reason being, no doubt, that the family is *the basic* social unit in any society. The second chapter of Genesis records that 'it is not good for man to be alone'. Man is by his very nature a social being, and the initial and most important source of social life for all people everywhere is the family. Indeed the first recorded command given to man was to 'be fruitful and multiply, and fill the earth'.

At the present time, family life is being challenged from a number of quarters. From all sides come attacks upon its authority, unity, purpose and intimacy. As the newspapers report from time to time, certain politicians, magistrates and educationists believe, not always without cause, that if parental influence over children can be lessened, they may have a better chance to direct young people into desirable paths. Some parents undermine their own authority by looking to other agencies to help to feed, teach and discipline their children. Pressures of work and many leisure-time attractions interrupt family unity and intimacy. Some critics argue that children and young people are over-indulged, while the aged are too often neglected. It may well be true of many homes that, as W. R. Niblett has said,[1] the family is more isolated today than previously, especially since daily life is so much more fragmented for large numbers of people. Certainly many enjoy less *family* activity – in work, social evenings, holidays and worship, for example – than did earlier generations. Perhaps, also, family culture is on the wane, as David Holbrook claimed in his book, *English for Maturity*.

One of the most serious causes of any decline that is occurring in the authority of the family can be found in the undermining of the sanctity of marriage. Unchastity before marriage, licence within it, and easier divorce – instances of which increase every year according to statistical surveys – all attack the sacredness of the marriage bond. The repercussions on children and young people, and therefore upon education, are very serious. In examining the Biblical teaching about parents and children therefore, it will be helpful first of all to glance at the main Christian ideas concerning marriage. We shall find that to adhere to the points which both the Old and the New Testament narratives emphasize is to lay a firm foundation for the tasks which face husbands and wives as parents.

Interestingly enough, in speaking about marriage the Biblical record does not mention the procreation of children. It concentrates exclusively on the significance of the relationship itself. In the first place it stresses that marriage is for the mutual help and encouragement of the two partners. 'I will make him a helper fit for him', says God of Adam in Genesis. In marriage one enters into a new status. The former dependent status as a son or daughter is relinquished as the new relationship is begun, although filial duties remain. Marriage is also a 'covenant' relationship established willingly and freely by the two concerned. The idea of such a covenant is far above the modern concept of a contract, and one of the sad features of much present-day discussion about marriage is the stress placed on the contractual aspect of the union. This is understandable at a time when divorce is distressingly frequent. The idea of marriage as a contract draws attention to the rights of each individual partner. But the Bible's emphasis is on *commitment*, the deliberately willed free giving of the whole self to another. This notion of commitment underlines the obligations of personal relationships, and it is impossible to conceive of such an act as anything but permanent and for all time, especially if children are to come from the union.

There is great mystery and wonder surrounding this union of two people. An inseparable unity – 'one flesh' – has been achieved. The New Testament likens this unity to the relationship between Christ and his church, a relationship which illustrates the structure that God has established for marriage. Married life realizes its full potential only within this structure. This places the husband at the head of the family, but both partners must love and cherish and honour each other since both are equal in the sight of God. God has bestowed honour and dignity upon the person and the office of both the wife and the husband. It is not so much mere natural attraction as consistent respect for the worth of each partner which establishes married life and love on an unshakeable basis. The tremendous significance of this relationship is thrown into even sharper relief in the Biblical condemnation of adultery. Scripture does not offer expedient reasons for trying to maintain a marriage. It concentrates on the solemn and mysterious nature of the covenant and union of husband and wife, adultery being seen as a violent rupturing of that bond and oneness, because it is an unnatural new union outside the original covenanted relationship.

Marriage, then, involves the closest physical and spiritual union of whole persons. It is a complete self-giving of each partner to the other. This is one reason why the entire New Testament emphasis is upon monogamy as the ideal to be followed. The

Old Testament too, while clearly showing the polygamous society common to the times – a state in which many ancient worthies lived – and while not specifically criticizing it, also shows the bad effects of such a system upon the individuals and children involved. Christian marriage is a relationship of love and respect between two people, neither of whom is in any way inferior to the other. It is a very secure union if properly honoured by both parties. Such love and security, respect and assurance form the ideal and only right setting for the birth and upbringing of children.

In 1963, a senior member of Her Majesty's Inspectorate wrote, in terms still applicable today, that 'the present theoretical position is very confused, and . . . whether we look at popular or professional wisdom, we do not detect a very clear or adequate notion of the nature and characteristics of children'.[2] Is the Bible's teaching about children any clearer?

The Bible offers us neither a fully documented psychological analysis of the young nor a set of basic pedagogical principles. What it does provide is a number of clear and definite statements concerning the nature and needs of children, and it reminds us of other aspects about them when referring to them in illustrations. The Christian doctrine of man recalls for us at once that, like all human beings, children are created in the 'image' of God. Spencer Leeson pointed out that because of this, all children are therefore 'capable of communion with God, they can approach Him in prayer and worship, they can be a vehicle of a revelation from Him and grow in His likeness, . . . and by His grace be made fellow workers with Him in His purpose'.[3] This triumphant statement leads us naturally to consider in more detail the Scriptural teaching about children.

Four preliminary points are worth making straight away. First, children are the gift of God: Eve is recorded as proclaiming, 'I have gotten a man (child) from the Lord.' The stories of Isaac and the Shunammite woman in the Old Testament, and of Elizabeth and Mary, the mother of Jesus, in the New underline this teaching. As the psalmist cries (Psalm 127), 'Lo, sons (children) are a heritage from the Lord, the fruit of the womb a reward. . . . Happy is the man who has his quiver full of them.' Secondly, children are very precious in God's sight. Christ's own dealings with the young are ample evidence of this. In the third place, children can be, and should be, dedicated to the Lord from the first. Samson, Samuel and John the Baptist are some who were so dedicated. Lastly, Matthew 18: 10 records Christ's statement that children enjoy God's special protection. As the American philosopher G. H. Clark once declared, 'Children do not belong to Caesar'.[4]

Although no detailed blueprint is provided, there is in the Bible much fruitful teaching about the nature of children, helpful suggestions and illustrations reinforcing the points made. Five main factors are worth listing. Most important of all, the Bible refutes categorically the view of Rousseau, and many others since his day, that children are born naturally good. It realistically asserts again and again in various ways that children are sinful from their earliest years. Genesis 8: 21 records God as saying that 'the imagination of man's heart is evil from his youth' (i.e. his earliest childhood). Some commentators believe that David was making exactly the same point in Psalm 51 when he acknowledged that 'in sin did my mother conceive me'. The Book of Proverbs comments that 'folly is bound up in the heart of the child'. In other words, that perversity of heart, mind, disposition and will which affects the deepest springs of the whole personality, that rebellious hostility to God, that bondage which enslaves all mankind, that unnatural condition to which all flesh is heir, is characteristic of the nature of every child as it is of every adult. This does not imply that children and adults cannot display natural virtues or support and work for civil righteousness. They can and do. Nevertheless it would be unrealistic folly to ignore the deep-seated existence of sin in every human heart.

A second important fact, one which educationists down the centuries have too often overlooked, is that children are naive, immature, lacking in discernment and of limited understanding. They are not adults in miniature. They have a life, language, values and an awareness of their own. Paul in 1 Corinthians 14 urged his readers not to be children in their thinking. Because they are naive and inexperienced, they can be easily led. Their ability to make sound judgments, and especially to decide for themselves about themselves, is suspect. It is children, not mature adults, who are likely to be 'tossed to and fro and carried about with every wind of doctrine' (Paul's words in Ephesians 4). As parents and teachers we need to comprehend the different stages of our children's development, since this will help to determine what and how we teach them. We must not demand of them understanding and behaviour which may be beyond their spiritual, mental and moral insight. Nor must we leave them to be guided by their own will. They need training in the way they should, not would, go. We must respect and recognize their limitations and not expect more of them than they are capable of giving, although, as Paul implies, they do develop and mature in time, with the right guidance. As he declared in 1 Corinthians 13: 'When I was a child, I spoke like a child, I thought like a child, I reasoned like a child; when I became a man, I gave up childish ways.'

Two further factors may be stated briefly. One is the recognition that children love play and make-believe and that this is part of their character. The illustrations used by different Biblical writers remind us of the fact. There is a delightful picture in Zechariah 8, of children playing in the streets of God-restored Jerusalem. Job refers to children dancing, and Christ illustrated a point in one of his sermons from children's play. The Bible also in several places reminds us that the young delight in their youth and their strength and vigour. The other point is that their actions reveal their nature, just like those of adults, in fact. As the Book of Proverbs (20: 11) puts it, 'even a child makes himself known by his acts, whether what he does is pure and right'.

A fifth point, already referred to in the quotation from Spencer

Leeson, is that children are capable of worship, praise and trust. There are many references in the Book of Psalms, and several in the Gospels, to children being engaged in praise and worship, whilst throughout the Bible there are numerous examples of children and young people taking part in acts of worship. Frequently in the Old Testament their presence at occasions for religious teaching, worship and ceremony was commanded by 'the law of the Lord'. Christ always encouraged children to come to him to hear his teaching and watch him at work. According to this evidence it is false to think, as some have done, that children are unable because of their youthfulness truly to have faith in God and worship and praise him properly.

To complete this part of the picture, one more component remains, the guileless simplicity and openness of children. Despite the presence of sin in their nature, they also display a charm and innocence which is very appealing. This is seen very clearly in their readiness to trust all who offer them affection and interest. It is such wholehearted, unreserved confidence and commitment which Christ declared to be the only way into the kingdom of heaven. We have to receive the kingdom of God as little children, to gain entrance. Their humility and ingenuous artlessness are not to be despised, for unless we trust and accept Christ with the humble readiness of children, he will have none of us.

Concerning the needs of children, four main tenets emerge from the Biblical narratives. Above all they need love and nursing, they need looking after, and they need the security that goes with love and care. The New Testament points out that they will find this love and security supremely in Christ, but that these blessings lie at the heart of true family life. A good home gives to children the assurance of belonging, and a sense of stability. It is a centre in which they can freely share their joys and pleasures. It is also a place of safety to which they can take their troubles, and a refuge from the fears and hurts of the world outside. A second thing children need and the Bible stresses is that they 'keep their way pure'. For only thus can they develop properly and fully.

They are to be loving and obedient, avoiding all that might defile or corrupt both themselves and – by their influence – others with whom they mix day by day. This is particularly stressed in certain psalms and in the Book of Proverbs. The third point follows obviously from what has been said. It is that all children need discipline and correction. Repeatedly one reads that a firm, orderly upbringing is essential for the young. Some people have mistakenly assumed that the Bible advocates repressive measures, with the rod and chastisement well to the fore. In fact, while recognizing that children will deserve and should receive punishment, including corporal punishment, from time to time, the Biblical emphasis is positive, based on real love and concern for the welfare of every child. The fourth need of the young which Biblical writers underline repeatedly, is for instruction. This is summed up in that verse from the Book of Proverbs quoted in a previous chapter. It states: 'Train up a child in the way he should go, and when he is old he will not depart from it.'

It is not unreasonable to suggest that all concerned with the upbringing of children and young people might take serious notice of all these points about the nature and needs of the young, especially in the context in which they are outlined. For it is against the whole background of Scripture that their full significance is seen. A great many parents and teachers recognize the relevance of most of the points, whether or not they know what the Bible has to say on these issues. Fully to accept and digest all that is said in the Biblical framework about the nature of children and their essential needs will help parents and teachers alike to plan and act realistically and positively. Perhaps the greatest problem is to know how to apply these principles in the ways that will most surely help growing children. Thanks to the work of many researchers, our understanding of the physical, mental and moral development of the young is increasing, and we must all use this knowledge as best we can. The Biblical reminders that children are dependent and vulnerable yet also created individuals, all of supreme worth, encourage a balanced approach which respects the integrity of every child and honours the God who made them.

Biblical writers do not leave the matter at this point, however. They have a number of further comments to make, notably about the duties and responsibilities of children. All children and young people within the community have certain definite obligations. They have particular allegiances to honour, and responsibilities to carry out which are suited to their nature and position in society. Most of all they should 'honour' their parents. This, the fifth of the Ten Commandments, is repeatedly stressed throughout the Bible. It involves respect, affection and obedience to one's father and mother throughout life. Closely linked with this is the duty to listen carefully to parental teaching. As the Book of Proverbs (1: 8) has it: 'Hear my son, your father's instruction, and reject not your mother's teaching.' This attention should also be paid to all instruction, whoever in authority may give it; the authority of parents in the Bible carries this natural extension.

When in the New Testament – in Ephesians 6: 1, and Colossians 3: 20 – children are instructed to obey their parents, the word translated 'obey' includes two main ideas. It means 'to do the bidding of' and 'to hearken submissively'. The same word is used of the wind and waves in the Gospel accounts of Christ stilling the storm, of unclean spirits submitting to the authority of Jesus (in Mark 1) and of Sarah obeying Abraham, as Peter describes this in his first letter. Just as humble, glad obedience through faith is the way of blessing in the Christian life, so it is the means to a happy childhood. The obedient child is living as God wishes him to live, and he can therefore share in the deep sense of rightness and harmony which such knowledge always provides. For he is free from the uncertainty and unease which plague every child who is not sure what is expected of him or who rebels against lawful authority. When a person knows where he stands in relation to authority he can relax. Children usually try from time to time to test authority, but they really want it to stand firm – because they want authority to be dependable and trustworthy.

When their trust proves well-founded, tension disappears and they become receptive to the truth and to all sound teaching.

Children should seek to gain insight, understanding and knowledge, especially concerning God himself. Throughout the Book of Proverbs, which directs so much of its teaching towards the young, they are urged to lay hold of truth and strive to become wise. A further point is related to all those so far mentioned. It is – a hard one this – to value discipline, correction and chastening. This is urged several times in the Bible, perhaps the best summary coming, appropriately enough some young people might think, in Lamentations 3 where we find the statement that 'it is good for a man that he bear the yoke in his youth'. Proverbs 6: 23 explains this: 'For the commandment is a lamp and the teaching a light, and the reproofs of discipline are the way of life.'

A factor of special importance is that children should reverence God and also all lawful human authority. Christ challenged his hearers to love him even more than their parents, whilst the Preacher (Ecclesiastes 12) asked children to remember their Creator in the days of their youth. In the Book of Proverbs there is the plea: 'My son, fear the Lord and the king, and do not disobey either of them.' Finally (Proverbs 3: 27), the young are exhorted to do good whenever they are able to do so. 'Do not withhold good from those to whom it is due, when it is in your power to do it.'

A number of warnings are also given to children about the consequences of disobedience, and failure to fulfil their responsibilities. Three that are particularly emphasized are worth mentioning. There is the folly of ignoring the teaching they are given – for 'he who ignores instruction, despises himself'. Again, sins against parents are extremely serious, and will be severely judged. In the third place, foolish, evil children are a source of great grief, not only to their parents but to the whole community.

To conclude this survey of the Bible's teaching on children, it also indicates in many places that various spiritual blessings are available to children as well as to adults. The most important of all is that God is always a refuge, especially for those who put their trust in him. He will be a Saviour and a Father to them, and will also teach them. Another point is that spiritual as well as natural wisdom is available to the youngest and most inexperienced as well as to more mature people. This is reiterated several times, particularly in the Book of Proverbs. Also, children can, do and will enjoy the blessings of the Holy Spirit. All these factors provide a corrective to those who have assumed that little spiritual awareness can be expected of children. They also provide encouragement to those engaged directly in the religious education of children.

What the Bible has to say about the duties and responsibilities of parents follows automatically from its teaching about the nature and needs of children. A fairly brief summary of its advice is possible, under four main headings. Obviously the central duty of parents is to surround their children with love and care. Love, sympathy and self-giving are at the heart of all family life. Christ pointed out more than once that compassion towards children is always rewarded. The love and attention they are given should both illustrate and as far as possible follow the example of God's care for his people.

A second main task of parents is to provide for their children. This includes a number of aspects. Provision of the material necessities of life for their children's daily welfare is one of these. Giving 'good gifts' to them is an obvious token of parental love. Neither should their spiritual needs be neglected. Parents should give their children security and protection, and companionship is important too. It is worth pointing out here that if parents faithfully carry out all the tasks that Biblical teaching expects of them as regards their family, then they will have to spend much time actually in the company of their children. Furthermore, special reference is made concerning prayer for the young, co-operating with God in his provision for them; the example of Job, for instance, is especially commendable in this respect.

One of the principal needs of children is for instruction. The Bible, in both Old and New Testaments, underlines the vital importance of the right teaching of the young, and this task is placed firmly upon the parents. Others can teach also, but fathers and mothers have the prime responsibility. This is not to suggest that they are expected to carry out full-scale educational programmes, but it is the parents' duty to ensure that their children receive a proper education, in which they themselves take an active part. They should be particularly concerned over the religious and moral education of their families. Paul's well-known instruction to his Ephesian readers illustrates the main drift of Biblical teaching. Urging consideration and good sense in the approach to young people, he wrote, 'Fathers, do not provoke your children to anger, but bring them up in the discipline and instruction of the Lord.' In particular, parents should teach their children to worship and praise God, to live humbly before him, and to learn and obey his word. Such teaching is essential. How can children in due course choose meaningfully and responsibly for themselves if they are ignorant of the choices before them? Over-dogmatic insistence or rigid indoctrination will not help them, however. Instruction and guidance must, of course, be clear and sympathetic to ensure true understanding. The aim is not meek and passive acceptance: each child has to be helped to make his own fully responsible decisions. This means, for adolescents especially, that the teaching they receive should explain and demonstrate rather than tell or compel.

The fourth responsibility laid upon parents is to discipline their children, to bring them up in a positive and orderly manner. This is greatly emphasized. It involves an insistence upon obedience, explicit guidance and correction, and punishment for wrong-doing, including physical punishment. Such discipline is a clear demonstration of the parents' love for their offspring. Whether they know it or not, children depend upon their parents to establish a pattern of order in their lives. Neglect of this duty has serious consequences for the family as a whole, and also for the society in which they live. For lack of discipline hampers moral development, and breeds insecurity, irresponsibility and inability to respect the needs and rights of others. Two verses in Proverbs 29 explain these points. Verse 15 states that 'the rod and reproof give wisdom, but a child left to himself brings shame to his mother'. Verse 17 says: 'Discipline your son, and he will give you rest; he will give delight to your heart.' The absence of clearly defined rules for children at home or anywhere else inevitably leads to behaviour, by parents and children alike, based on the impulse of the moment or the variable moods of personal feeling. An equally unsatisfactory alternative is to overload young people with petty restrictions. Yet children must have some regulations if they are not to grow up warped or shiftless or neurotic. To maintain these rules consistently demands real willpower, but the effort is well worth while and will earn the respect and gratitude of the young.

As with children, certain special warnings are also given to adults. The most strongly worded of these concern those who cause children to stumble or go astray. Christ himself bluntly warned his hearers about this when he said that it would be better for such people to have a millstone hung round their necks and be drowned. Parents have a very great influence over their children, far greater than any school or teacher: children so readily imitate their fathers and mothers in what they say and do. Parents should be particularly careful not to encourage children to worship 'false gods', like money, public esteem, pleasure and power. A second warning, repeated many times in the Old Testament is that the sins of the parents are visited on the children. The point just made that children imitate their parents is one illustration of this. But also, children frequently suffer as a result of wrong done by their fathers and mothers.

As was noted earlier, Ephesians 6: 4 warns parents not to 'provoke their children to anger'. The word used here means 'to irritate or to anger beyond measure', to exasperate and make them resentful. The word translated 'provoke' in Colossians 3: 21

literally means 'to rouse to strife'. Pointless teasing, mindless sarcasm, inconsistent or half-hearted instruction, nagging, indecisive discipline can all irritate and upset children. It is unfair and unloving to treat them like this, and it can have grave consequences. Under such treatment, children quickly lose heart. The Amplified Version of the Bible's translation of the Colossians verse effectively explains the point: 'Do not provoke, or irritate or fret your children – do not be hard on them or harass them, lest they become discouraged and sullen and morose and feel inferior and frustrated; do not break their spirit.'

Two other warnings should be mentioned. The first stresses the danger of mixed marriages. In this respect the Old Testament is referring to marriages between God's people, Israel, and the people of other tribes and nations who worship other gods and do not serve the God of Israel. In the New Testament the warning means that Christians should not marry unbelievers. In both cases, to enter into such contracts means that one is trying to achieve an impossibility: for unity is impossible where the spiritual centre of one personality has no correspondence with that of the other. How can light have fellowship with darkness, Paul asked. The outcome would be spiritually disastrous and so adversely affect the whole relationship. The Scriptures are full of illustrations of the unfortunate results of such marriages both for parents and children.

The second warning is more of a command than a prophecy of doom. It is the constant reminder to parents that their own obedience to God and his law is as vital as that of their children. They should live out in their lives the principles they teach to their families. To do so is a mark of proper Christian discipleship and an embodiment of true authority. The faithful following out of God's will results in well-being for one's children as well as for oneself. It is a basis from which the young gain rich blessings and an example to inspire and help them in their walk through life. As the Book of Proverbs comments, 'A righteous man who walks in his integrity – blessed are his sons after him.'

In our society at the present time, the primary responsibility for the education of our children still rests upon the parents. Lack of time, of adequate opportunities, of knowledge and of necessary equipment, makes it impossible for most parents to undertake the whole education of their sons and daughters. Nevertheless it is still perfectly possible for parents to provide the kind of upbringing stressed in the Bible. It is a natural duty for parents to love and care for their young and to see that they are properly educated. This education includes teaching them to know about and understand Christianity, encouraging them to worship, and having a general concern for their spiritual welfare. Parents, like teachers, have to face the fact that their influence on their children may sometimes be resented at the time, and yet may bear fruit eventually – perhaps many years later. They need to realize too that their effect on their families is determined much more by the sort of people they are than by any explicit instruction they may give.

The whole emphasis of Jewish education, following the Biblical pattern, was not on the child's future in the world of work, though this was not neglected. It was primarily an education in God's laws for right living. Parents in the twentieth century can still follow this lead, as they instruct their children in the law and worship of God, and train them in obedience, self-control and the gradual assumption of responsibility. Parents can also set a godly example themselves as well as providing loving discipline and an attractive, positive environment for their children. William Lillie makes an interesting point when he comments that the common root of 'truth' (*emeth*), and 'faithfulness' (*emurah*) is used concerning a mother's care. 'The vivid picture of the constancy and steadfastness of the parent to her child lurks behind the Old Testament conception of faithfulness.'[5] Also, E. B. Castle reminds us, concerning the Jewish boy, that 'what was binding upon him, was binding on his parents also; so life made sense'.[6] This could be just as true for all children in this country today, not merely those from Christian homes. Lastly, the Biblical teaching about parents and children has real relevance to teachers too, since they are all – from this author's viewpoint at least – to a certain extent *in loco parentis*. This will be considered in the final chapter of the book.

REFERENCES TO CHAPTER SEVEN

[1] W. R. Niblett, *Christian Education in a Secular Society*, OUP, 1960, p. 6.
[2] J. Blackie, *Good Enough for the Children*, Faber & Faber, 1963, p. 51.
[3] Spencer Leeson, *Christian Education*, Longmans Green, 1947, p. 116.
[4] G. H. Clark, *A Christian Philosophy of Education*, W. B. Eerdmans, 1946, p. 186.
[5] W. Lillie, *Studies in New Testament Ethics*, Oliver and Boyd, 1961, p. 6.
[6] E. B. Castle, *Moral Education in Christian Times*, Allen and Unwin, 1958.

Chapter Eight

THE CONTENT OF EDUCATION

What we actually teach our children at home and at school depends on a number of factors. Most of the instruction given by parents is incidental and goes on for most of the time, any formal teaching tending in most cases to be spasmodic and irregular, usually taking place only when an apparent need arises. Children are taught social habits and attitudes, and they have a certain amount of moral training. They also acquire the particular values and standards of the home and neighbourhood to which the family group belongs and, to a lesser extent, of the general society in which they live. The content of their education at school has tended to be determined by tradition and the requirements of examinations. Only at the present time is a detailed study being made of the curriculum in both primary and secondary schools, with research being done by various bodies into the content and teaching methods of particular subjects.

What are Christians doing about the curriculum? Some are taking part in the various research programmes just mentioned. Are Christian teachers in general examining what they teach from a Christian point of view? There are not many subjects on school timetables where this would be impossible. Are there any Christian considerations which it would be reasonable to apply to questions of educational content? Indeed there are. Yet for too long now, Christians in education have appeared to assume that, apart from religious knowledge, there is very little of a specifically Christian nature that they can contribute to the content of education. Many would agree that at the level of general educational theory, Christian principles can and should be applied. When considering subject syllabuses, however, it seems that Christians can have little or nothing to say. But this is not true.

The Bible is definitely relevant when we consider what children should be taught. This does not mean that it is to be regarded as an educational textbook, even though it may well supply much of the main content of religious education lessons. Nor does it mean that the schools should be teaching something called Christian physics or geography or moral studies, as opposed to other kinds of physics, geography and ethics. There are no such subjects as Christian biology, or mathematics, or home economics. Nevertheless as we have seen, the Biblical doctrine of man, its teaching about cultural gifts, about wisdom and knowledge, and about the needs of children, can all affect the content of the education of every child. For instance it has been said before in this book that we must try to impart natural knowledge and wisdom and encourage the development of all skills and talents, if each new generation is to continue man's task of controlling the earth and having dominion over it. And because of the importance of every created human being, the all-round development of every single pupil must be borne in mind.

It might be objected that we take account as best we can of all these factors anyway. We do try to give our children an all-round education. Most of the subjects taught in school are clearly differentiated, having their own criteria and aims. Each one demands its own specific, in-built approach which students must understand and follow if they are to achieve mastery in each particular field. School subjects are not, in their criteria or methods noticeably dependent upon Christian principles or pre-suppositions. Therefore Christian and non-Christian educationists can work harmoniously together at all levels, and pursue many of the same aims in doing so. Why should we then have to seek out any Scriptural backing for what we do in school, especially as the Bible does not provide a blue-print on education?

Once more the Christian answer is that the Biblical teaching concerning God and man and the created order undergirds the whole process of education as of life. We need to acknowledge this both in theory and in practice. To do so will help to guarantee two vital consequences. Firstly we are more likely to protect the true meaning of personality. If we remember that all children are God-created beings, deserving the deepest care and respect, we shall more effectively resist the temptation to disparage or neglect some of them, and we shall try harder to give them that all-round education they all deserve. Secondly, our approach, if tempered by Christian insight, will be more balanced and realistic. For we shall recognize and take account of the limitations both of human nature and of the education our children receive. Educational thinking must be 'salted' with Christian principles about man and his world. Christian standards and values must permeate both what we teach and the methods we adopt, then they will act as a preservative of the good and wholesome, and as a defence against that which is unjust or can corrupt. Christian values will have a most positive influence for good on the tone and ethos of any school. One clearly practical outcome of a Christian approach to the curriculum will be the persistent asking of certain key questions. Is the subject-matter being taught in the different lessons appropriately nourishing? How will it affect the children who receive it? Will it, and the ways in which it is presented, promote proper attitudes – to the particular subject itself, to other subjects, to other people? How far do the ideas and values being promulgated harmonize with Christian teaching, and how can pupils be helped to understand any differences that may exist between viewpoints? It is not suggested that all these questions are *Christian* questions, but that they are queries which Christians in particular ought regularly to ask.

Furthermore, if we approach the different domains of knowledge with Christian standards and values in mind, these criteria will inevitably influence what we select and reject, what we emphasize and spend time on in class and what we teach in more incidental fashion. Nothing of real importance would be neglected. It would be unjustifiable to conclude that the outcome of such an approach would be a narrowly restricted curriculum of a mainly religious nature. Most of what children are now taught in school would continue to feature in subject syllabuses. Its presence would not be affected by religious considerations. What has been stated earlier in this book about cultural gifts and wisdom and knowledge reinforces this fact. Nor should one conclude that the curriculum would be heavily biased from a Christian viewpoint. No worthwhile teacher favours indoctrination, and open-ended methods are essential, especially where opinions and personal beliefs are concerned. In any case Christianity has regard for all truth, and does not fear any counter-opinions. It demands openness to the evidence and is as much the enemy of prejudice as of cynicism and indifference. A Christian approach to the content of education will bring its own distinctive atmosphere and style, a difference of tone and perhaps of temperament, to quote again some of C. S. Lewis's terms.

Scriptural exhortations include certain specific suggestions about the content of a child's education at home and at school. These proposals are directed mainly at parents and the church, and in the Old Testament at the national leaders also. Theirs is the prime responsibility. But if our schools today are to help cater for all our children's educational needs, then they also share something of this task, along with all their other duties.

'Teaching' in the Bible has at least two main subjects, the nature and purpose of God and the nature and condition of man. The first is concerned with 'law', history, religion and ethics – God's word, works, worship and moral standards, and the second with the needs of the individual person. Certain general advice is also given. Each of these details is worth comment.

In the first place, both the Old and New Testaments emphasize that children should be taught the main points of the 'law', the word of God. This would involve learning by heart, writing out, and meditating upon various passages, as well as listening to readings and expositions. God's revelation is most precious and should be studied with great diligence. As Moses reminded his people, 'the secret things belong to the Lord our God; but the things that are revealed belong to us and to our children for ever, that we may do all the words of this law.' The heart of this teaching was summed up in the Shema (Deuteronomy 6: 4–7), which was the first piece of Scripture that all Jewish children had to learn: 'Hear, O Israel: The Lord our God is one Lord; and you shall love the Lord your God with all your heart, and with all your soul, and with all your might. And these words which I command you this day shall be upon your heart; and you shall teach them diligently to your children, and shall talk of them when you sit in your house, and when you walk by the way, and when you lie down, and when you rise.'[2]

The same commands were equally stressed in the New Testament, especially by Christ himself, who underlined the immutability and permanence of his teaching and the importance of 'searching the Scriptures'. Paul's words in 1 Timothy 3 emphasize the profitability of the Scriptures for instruction, reproof, correction and training in righteousness, 'so that the man of God may be complete and proficient, well-fitted and thoroughly equipped for every good work' (Amplified Version).

Secondly, it was imperative for each new generation of Israel to know what God had performed on their behalf. For the Hebrew people the most obvious example was their deliverance from Egypt and the thraldom of Pharaoh. Since New Testament times, for Christians and for all men, it is the birth, life, teaching, death and resurrection of Jesus Christ that would be cited. God's mighty works are therefore to be declared to all people, and not least to the young. Indeed this is part of the gospel teaching of the church. For the works of God, like his law, reveal something of his nature, those aspects about which he wishes mankind to know. Direct teaching concerning his revealed nature is likewise called for, in addition to accounts of what he has done in creation and providence, since children need to be taught 'to revere and worshipfully fear the Lord'.

Thirdly, children need to learn to worship God. The experience of being present at services and ceremonies when worship takes place should not be denied them. It would be very unfortunate if at school, for instance, religious assemblies were abolished. Admittedly their form, timing, duration and purpose require great care, but sensitively presented, they can be educationally invaluable. There are numerous examples in the Bible of children, including Christ as a child, being present at religious festivals, as well as Sabbath and other special occasions. As the psalmist wrote: 'Kings of the earth and all peoples, princes and all rulers of the earth! Young men and maidens together, old men and children! Let them praise the name of the Lord.' A close link can exist between the teaching process and adult obedience to the laws and commanded religious ceremonies. The child's curiosity may be roused and he will ask questions. The way is then open for a specific lesson. As some verses in Deuteronomy 6 put the point, 'When your son asks you in time to come, "What is the meaning of the testimonies and the statutes and the ordinances which the Lord our God has commanded you?", then you shall say to your son, "We were Pharaoh's slaves in Egypt; and the Lord brought us out of Egypt with a mighty hand . . .' and so on. One further point. The practical experience of services of worship helps to reinforce understanding of the precepts taught at home and in class.

Fourthly, there is the moral training of the young. The Bible evidences a deep concern for the needs of every individual person as it sets out the moral standards which God demands of mankind. At all points, it emphasizes both the hearing and the doing of God's word. Here is the active principle of education. For education, like religion, is not merely an academic pursuit but is concerned with a life to be lived. It is the consistent Scriptural view that indirect moral training is not enough. Direct, regular, detailed instruction is also essential. The idea that morality, in the sense of a clear framework of moral standards, is caught, not taught, is not acceptable. It is 'caught' just because it is taught as well as practised. It cannot be taken for granted that children will automatically know what is right or wrong or that they will all inevitably acquire this knowledge as they grow up. Passage after passage in the Bible constantly underlines the need for children to obey God, and their parents, and all lawful authority. Equally they emphasize active righteous conduct in every department of life. Both the positive and the negative aspects of morality are to be dealt with, as the Bible's own teaching exemplifies. Such a fully balanced approach ensures that the instruction given will be clear and all-inclusive. It is principally but not exclusively the task of the parents to ensure this. Where the schools can help most is in teaching their pupils to know and understand moral precepts and their practical implications.

Finally, many verses in the Bible endorse, especially by example and implication, the study of the knowledge and beauties of this world. Children and young people are to seek out wisdom and apply it to their situation. As was mentioned in an earlier chapter, some of the most eminent men referred to in the Bible were scholars of great ability and learning. Their wisdom is commended as well as their faithfulness to God and their powers of leadership and teaching. The general principle that is given in Scripture concerning, among other things, natural wisdom and knowledge, is to be found in Philippians 4. 'Whatever is true, honourable, just, pure, lovely, gracious, if there is any excellence, if there is anything worthy of praise, think about these things'. The word 'think' here means 'to search out a thing diligently by comparing one with another'. This entails detailed study as well as careful meditation. It is also worth repeating that it is acknowledged in the Bible that the content of education must be partly determined by the needs and level of the learners. The advice in the Book of Proverbs to train children 'in the way they should go', and the New Testament principle of feeding with milk or strong meat according to capacity, illustrate this in their different ways.

Little is said in the Bible concerning how to teach, but the methods used by many teachers, supremely by Christ himself, are a demonstration of them. For instance they used stories, topical illustrations, visual aids and dramatic enactment, direct explanation and exhortation. They drew on the experience of those being taught, awakened their curiosity, used careful questioning, and encouraged learning by heart – still a worthwhile exercise despite the distaste some feel for it as a teaching method.

A careful study of the teaching techniques of Jesus would be profitable for anyone, regardless of the beliefs he might hold. He captured the interest and attention of his audience whether they were friendly or hostile. He led his hearers on to essential issues and away from irrelevant or lesser matters. He answered questions by asking another to deepen the issue, or by making the questioner answer his own question. He encouraged and rebuked and exhorted and expounded. He used the experience and knowledge of his listeners. He illustrated what he was saying in simple but telling language, with captivating stories and word pictures. He adapted his approach to meet individual natures and needs. His concern for every person showed through all his dealings with people. To note these methods is indeed to learn how to teach. What is more, Jesus' teaching provides the perfect answer to those who argue that the positive presentation of a belief is incompatible with the pupil's freedom of thought. Jesus taught, as even his enemies acknowledged, 'as one having authority'. Yet he could never be accused of indoctrination. He never rode roughshod over his listeners' independence of mind. Rather, his teaching aimed at stimulating his hearers' own mental activity. That is to say, his teaching was teaching, not propaganda.

Perhaps as good a summary of how to prepare and present one's material as can be found in the Bible is offered in the example of the Preacher. We are told in the last chapter of Ecclesiastes that although everything under the sun is vanity, 'because the Preacher was wise, he still taught the people knowledge; yea, he gave good heed' (with concentrated care and attention), 'and sought out' (with diligent enquiry and research) 'and set in order' (preparing and presenting his material in a clear and logical arrangement) 'many proverbs' (having ample variety of subject matter). He also 'sought to find out acceptable – pleasing – words' (suitable material, understandably and attractively expressed). His reminder that 'much study is a weariness of the flesh' warns of man's limitations and encourages a realistic attitude both to one's particular subject and to education as a whole.

The Christian approach to the content of education has its most valuable and most obviously practical part to play in the development of attitudes. Personal values emerge not only in one's evaluation of particular situations, and one's selection of material, but in the whole way in which one is teaching. In some subjects, mathematics or geography, for instance, a person's Christian commitment may make little difference to the presentation of the subject. Where such commitment is clearly relevant, as in history or religious education, there must be no attempt at indoctrination. It is part of every teacher's task to help children to develop a willing desire to consider *all* sides of a situation. To suppress any relevant points of view, Christian or otherwise, is to encourage prejudice or distortion rather than impartiality and objectivity. The Christian approach demands rigorous integrity, honesty, openness, and real respect and concern for the truth and for the ideas and feelings of others. It will assist children to value what is traditional and conventional as well as what is new and spontaneous. By promoting freedom in study the Christian approach will underline the importance of rules and method for helping to achieve that very freedom and for using it responsibly.

In bringing the Christian approach to bear upon creative activities, we shall be encouraging children to form and develop their feelings and ideas through experience, and this will in turn help them to assess these feelings and ideas. We shall encourage them to express their personalities and ideas creatively in order to achieve something worthwhile, and not in order to revel in self-glorification. For it *is* worthwhile to learn to capture scenes, moods or ideas and to express and communicate them to others. In self-expression one should be expressing more than just oneself; otherwise self-expression is in danger of becoming self-assertion, and this is a danger the teacher should guard against. Christians most of all should want to promote humility in the face of greatness and in achieving success in study. A final sign of the influence of Christian attitudes upon the curriculum would be that teachers and pupils alike would consciously appreciate and be grateful for the riches of creation revealed in each area of study.

At a fundamental level, knowledge can be differentiated into only a limited number of areas between which one can clearly discriminate. Such fields of knowledge are the mathematical, scientific, religious, moral, historical, philosophical and perhaps the aesthetic. Most enlightened educationists, whether Christian or not, would argue that the core curriculum of any school should include aspects of these realms of knowledge and truth. The only way we have any right to teach any subject is to tell the truth as far as we can discern it. It is every specialist teacher's task to discern truth from error, and to help his pupils to do likewise. Truth affects the whole person, and the whole person must be catered for – the emotional, physical, moral and spiritual, as well as intellectual, development of all pupils. In many subjects the training of head and heart go together. Young minds require exercise and guidance; pre-digested knowledge will not help them very much to think for themselves. But although head and heart go together, we should beware of the approach of a curriculum which glorifies either knowledge or personality. Nor is there any special hierarchy of courses. No one school subject is more important than any other, in a programme which aims to offer a general education. A comment by G. H. Clark is worth adding. He argues that 'the school system that ignores God teaches its pupils to ignore God and this is not neutrality; it is the worst form of antagonism, for it judges God to be unimportant and irrelevant in human affairs.'[1]

It was mentioned earlier that each area of study has its own criteria and methods, which are not determined by particular religious presuppositions and principles, but by the nature of the subjects themselves. Nevertheless Biblical teaching about God and his purpose for mankind should not be completely ignored in the presentation of different subjects. This is not to advocate that every lesson is a kind of religious education lesson, but just to point out that certain comments and explanations from the Christian point of view, are relevant to the teaching of some subjects.

In a denominational school or college, this is perhaps not difficult to arrange. A. B. Sackett has asserted that 'the curriculum of a Christian education is ruled by the conviction that truth is one. Each branch of man's investigation of his environment . . . is a searching out of the thoughts of God; each is a religious and worshipful activity'.[2] D. C. Wyckoff similarly argues that 'the curriculum of Christian education sees the area of God, man, nature and history in a comprehensive way and in a Christian perspective'.[3] The maintained school situation is more complex. Yet even there it is quite possible – indeed it is absolutely essential – to present the Christian perspective for children to consider in a reasonable way. Just as in religious education lessons children are taught, without any attempt to compel belief, to know about and understand Christianity, so in other subjects where Christian teaching has relevance, the Christian view can be stated along with others. Furthermore, the assumptions and pre-suppositions which lie behind particular subjects can often be assessed in the light of Christian teaching. The theory of evolution in biology, the idea of progress in history and social theory, and the belief in free will in ethics are just three examples which might be chosen for analysis with pupils capable of such work. All this assumes that Christian teachers will have done their homework, and that there are textbooks and other writings available which explain clearly and objectively the Christian arguments relevant to different aspects of the curriculum. It assumes also that all Christians in education are, to borrow Harry Blamires' phrase, 'thinking Christianly' about their work.

It may be worthwhile at this point to glance at particular features of school curricula, even though comment must be brief, and therefore somewhat superficial. History is one subject where the Christian world view has something definite to offer. It is not simply that in our study of Western civilization we are bound to consider the rise, progress and influence of Christianity. Christian teaching about man, and the providence of God, can influence our approach to the past as to the future. Man's true nature and significance, as the Christian gospel declares, can only be realized from a vantage point outside time. The Bible offers this eternal perspective. From this standpoint we can perceive something of the *meaning* of history; it has also been given the greatest significance by the fact that God intervened in time in the person of Jesus Christ. Biblical authors give us a true account of time. The world is going somewhere, from a given start to a definite conclusion. This truth, along with the fact that God became man in Christ, gives a significance to all man's actions in the different periods of history that no other world view, and particularly the one that claims that man evolved by blind chance, can possibly provide. This certainty about time and its purposeful on-going movement is rooted in the doctrines of creation and divine providence. Biblical teaching therefore reinforces our sense of the importance of history, and at the same time offers an interpretation of all history. Incidentally, what is sometimes called 'Deuteronomic History' – the period from the Book of Judges to the end of 2 Kings – is the oldest piece of consecutive historical writing in existence. Six centuries are presented as a meaningful sequence and interpreted according to certain religious and political views. For the Biblical writers regarded history with the utmost seriousness. It is highly significant that the Jews thought historically where the Greeks thought metaphysically. To put it differently, truth was, for the Jews, incarnational; for the Greeks, transcendental. It is no accident that the incarnation is central in Christian teaching nor that the incarnation took place among the people who thought historically and incarnationally about reality. Where the Greeks speculated about the nature of ultimate reality, the Jews thought in terms of 'This hath God *done*'.

Before they leave school therefore, as many pupils as possible should have been helped to understand these things, and have discussed this and other approaches to the past. It will help them to put in perspective the detailed analyses of particular periods and people which they may have undertaken. It will promote that 'sense of history' which teachers of this subject wish their pupils to acquire.

Science is another subject where the Christian perspective is enlightening. Professor D. M. Mackay once wrote that 'science pursued humbly and consistently according to its own principles is a discipline on the side of the angels'.[4] Certainly the intensive study of nature is essential if man is to fulfil the command to subdue the earth. Such study should also help men to realize how to use and conserve the riches of the earth, and to recognize the dangers of squandering its resources for selfish ends. Some scientists who are Christians have said that scientific study has helped them to grasp something of the immanence and transcendence of God. The Christian faith believes that science can help us to understand the conditions for life in our world. The Christian doctrine of providence undergirds all scientific study, for instance in the assumption of order, which is one of science's articles of faith. Another example is in the assumption of constancy – which for Christians is based on God's promise in Genesis 8 that as long as the earth remains, seedtime and harvest, cold and heat, summer and winter, day and night will not cease. It is no accident that the main advances of science and technology have taken place within Christendom. No other civilization has taken the phenomenal world seriously enough to study it consistently and in detail in search of truth. Scientific study is one sure way in which man can assert himself over his world. This has advantages and also moral dangers, but the knowledge that it is God's creation we are investigating helps to encourage that humility of which Professor Mackay spoke. A further point with regard to science is that the discoveries made by scientists usually have moral implications as they affect people's lives. Here again the Christian point of view will have something significant to contribute.

The need to educate children in values and aesthetic awareness as well as in skills and factual knowledge is readily acknowledged by most people. Professor W. R. Niblett once wrote that the 'bias in the secondary school is in favour of studies which neither involve much reckoning with personal experience nor much ability to experience at some depth'. Reality is apprehended through feeling and aesthetic appreciation as well as cognitively. The skill of the artist is among the wonders of creation, adding to man's life an extra splendour and delight, as well as providing relief from the daily round. It has often been said that creative activity is an aspect of the fact that man has been created in God's image. Basil Willey has written that 'art without faith loses vision and direction, becomes capricious, arbitrary or chaotic; and the enjoyment of it similarly becomes an affair of momentary and disconnected thrills, ecstasies or stupors'.[5] How true his words are has been clearly demonstrated in certain forms of modern art, and in *musique concrète*. Christian insight can inform and guide the artist in his choice of subject-matter and increase his own sympathetic understanding and that of his audience as well.

When we are trying to discover and teach something about values, literature is a very great help. Literature, properly read and taught, should bring pleasure for its own sake. But it should do more than that, for literature communicates more than just itself. Ancient writers realized this. The old myths, legends and folk tales had a didactic as well as entertaining purpose. They introduced the young to the ethical inheritance of the race or group. The best literature has always done this. It offers some training in moral judgment. It can give a greater understanding of man, providing insight into his make-up and motives. It can face children also with problems concerning the meaning and purpose of life. Much great literature, from George Herbert and Bunyan to T. S. Eliot and C. S. Lewis, to cite examples that span the periods most commonly studied in English lessons, is imbued with Christian values, as well as maintaining the highest literary standards. The Bible itself has frequently given a lead with its magnificent poetry and skilful story-telling. Both in content and purpose it rejects the unsatisfactory doctrine of art for art's sake. It demonstrates in its finest writing some of the criteria of great literature – form and content combining perfectly to create a work of art which is intellectually, morally and spiritually edifying as well as aesthetically pleasing.

Before leaving the subject of aesthetic values, one question might be briefly aired. St Paul urged the Philippians to think about the true, the just, the pure and the lovely. But how does one decide what is excellent, lovely or praiseworthy? If the question is one of morality, the Bible provides the standards on which judgments should be based. In the aesthetic sphere, Scripture does not pronounce definitively. Although there will probably be general agreement in most cases, different people may arrive at different answers concerning what is good or beautiful in art, music, or sculpture. Nonetheless, since much in the aesthetic realms has moral overtones and implications, Biblical teaching about the pure, true and excellent provides standards which act as both guide and safeguard to creative artists and those who study their work, especially as regards subject-matter.

Upon what other fields of education does Christianity bring light to bear? There is much talk today about general or liberal studies in school, and also about moral education. It has already been stressed that the Bible advocates direct moral instruction, and there is certainly a strong case for specific moral education lessons especially at the secondary school level. Scriptural teaching would suggest that pupils might study the nature of society, and the problems and responsibilities of work, leisure and adult life generally. They also need opportunities to exercise responsibility, perhaps through social service, in addition to discussing fundamental issues. The full development of their physical powers is important too. They need healthy bodies and some knowledge of bodily structure and function, if they are to carry out their duties with vigour, both in youth and as adults. Christian teaching insists on an all-round education for every child, although the

Biblical command to subdue the earth lends backing for the idea of specialist study also. Neither should be stressed at the expense of the other.

Concerning general studies, and also the thematic and integrated studies now in vogue in some quarters, little that is specifically Christian can be said. Here again Christian insight and values, where pertinent, might enlighten and guide thinking about the choice of subject-matter and the time to be spent on it. Integrated studies can be very valuable as long as distinctive fields of knowledge are not blurred, confused or neglected in the process. General studies lessons often provide a forum for the discussion of controversial issues. At such times the teacher usually acts as neutral chairman. It would be his responsibility to ensure that adequate factual information was available, that every relevant point of view was fairly treated, and that the implications, Christian and non-Christian, of different conclusions were made clear.

E. H. Harbison has said that 'the cure for the divorce of liberal learning from Christianity is not the Christianization of the content of the curriculum but more learned and committed Christians in liberal education, shedding what light they can, in humility and devotion to truth, on the wider meaning of the subjects they teach'.[6] There is no doubt that the Biblical perspective helps to clarify issues and to set up standards which make for a positive approach to the content of education. It helps also to relate all the various activities together and thus to give a unifying purpose to what takes place at home and at school in the upbringing of the young. It recognizes the value of all valid studies and acknowledges gladly and thankfully the contributions made in these fields by all, whatever their personal beliefs might be. It therefore helps to ensure that the gifts of creation and culture are available to all, to the enrichment of the personal life of individuals and of the collective life of the whole society. A curriculum based on a defensible theory of knowledge and offering the content and perspective which the Bible requires, should provide the coherent, balanced and wholesome education which all our children ought to have. One of the tasks of every Christian teacher therefore, is to demonstrate this fact as far as possible both in the teaching of his own subject and in general discussions about the content of education. This is demanding work. Yet clear-thinking people who know what they believe and who can see the implications of their standpoint for their work, are likely to make the best teachers. For they can stretch young minds, and more readily recognize the limitations of both their pupils and their subject.

REFERENCES TO CHAPTER EIGHT

[1] G. H. Clark, *A Christian Philosophy of Education*, W. B. Eerdmans, 1946, p. 80.

[2] A. B. Sackett, 'Christian Education', in R. E. Davies, ed., *An Approach to Christian Education*, Epworth Press, 1957, p. 26.

[3] D. C. Wyckoff, 'The Curriculum and the Church School', in M. J. Taylor, ed., *Religious Education: a Comprehensive Survey*, Abingdon, 1960, p. 102.

[4] D. M. MacKay, 'Science and . . .', *Religion in Education*, Vol. XXVII, No. 1., Autumn 1959, p. 22.

[5] B. Willey, 'Christianity and Literature', in *An Approach to Christian Education*, Epworth Press, 1957, p. 121.

[6] E. H. Harbison, 'Liberal Education and Christian Education', in E. Fuller, ed., *The Christian Idea of Education*, Yale University Press, 1957, pp. 68–69.

Chapter Nine
CHRISTIAN MORALITY AND EDUCATION

What the Bible says on the subject of morality is undeniably applicable to the upbringing of children and young people. Clear ethical standards are set out which apply to the whole of man's personal and social life. The most significant part of Christian teaching is concerned with man's relationship to God and to his fellow human beings. Despite this, and the fact that every school is directly involved in the moral education of its pupils, Christian teachers have not sufficiently emphasized the relevance of Biblical moral instruction to educational theory and practice. For this teaching should not be confined to religious knowledge lessons. Christians should be pointing out that it applies everywhere in the educational field, and especially in the whole life of every school.

Unfortunately, many people today are ignorant and confused about Christian morality. Most children are now growing up unaware of moral standards based on the law of God. Familiarity with Biblical concepts and recognition of Christian influence is fast disappearing. The main reason for this lack of understanding is that people no longer read their Bibles regularly and intelligently. The Christian church itself must bear some of the blame for this situation. Not only is there a dearth of expository preaching, so that Christian congregations are not properly instructed. There is also the fact that Christians themselves do not speak with one voice on moral issues but are guilty of contradictory teaching. Some dismiss Old Testament moral teaching as 'sub-Christian', or ignore it altogether. Others select certain parts of the New Testament and reject the rest, arguing for instance that the teaching of St Paul conflicts with that of Christ. Others again do not base their ideas on Biblical morality at all. This should not be. As careful reading will show, the Old and New Testaments present consistent and definite moral standards which it is vital, for personal and public health and well-being, that everyone should understand. No other source provides such practical and all-embracing guidance. Christians in education, therefore, have a special responsibility to make this teaching known, particularly when people are so uninformed and perplexed. The aim of this chapter is consequently threefold. First, to consider briefly the current confusion about morality, and then to discuss the nature and purpose of Biblical morality. Lastly we shall try to illustrate the relevance of Christian moral teaching at the classroom level.

All human beings possess a sense of right and wrong. This sense appears to be innate, an intrinsic part of human nature, and to be analogous in certain respects to the direct perception of the external world by the senses. It also seems to have something in common with the rational perception of truth, and the consciousness of personal identity. It is possible for a person deliberately to stifle his moral consciousness, and for unscrupulous or misguided people to warp and confuse the ethical awareness of others. But for all practical purposes it seems to be established that moral perception and judgment are an essential part of what is meant by being truly human.

Just as moral consciousness is, in the created world, unique to human experience, so moral judgments are distinctive, forming a logically self-contained area of discourse. Some of these judgments further appear to have a certain independence, being neither conditioned nor controlled by the will of man. They make people generally feel conscious of liability and responsibility, and of obligation to act in accordance with the sanctions that they incorporate. The concept of moral law follows from this, and these moral judgments appear to have some sort of authority over men. The conviction of moral responsibility which these laws instil makes people believe themselves to be accountable to an authority above both themselves and society. All men live under a higher law, whether they like it or not and whether they obey it or not. Christians argue that man's moral consciousness, and his feeling of being answerable to an authority above himself and his world, stems from his creation in the image of God. His consciousness of right and wrong distinguishes him from the other creatures, making him the one earthly creature who can be fittingly addressed in moral terms by his Creator, under whose law he is meant to live in complete trust and dependence.

Attempts of various kinds are always being made to influence man's behaviour. In all walks of life there are rules, customs and habits which guide or prescribe as regards the ways we act in different situations. The most obvious are the laws and customs of the society in which we live. But there are many other examples in addition to these. There are the rules and regulations imposed by a school or a business firm upon its members, or the trade requirements and codes of conduct established by different crafts and professional bodies. There are the manners that one is expected to adopt as a member of a particular family or group or class. The rules of the game, and the habits associated with special ritual and ceremonial activities are two further illustrations. Public opinion exerts a great influence on the conduct of all the members of any society. The teachings of the different religions aim to affect the attitudes and actions of their adherents, and finally there are a variety of moral codes, some religious and some secular, all of which make claims upon our behaviour, both private and public.

More and more people today, the young especially, are questioning the various moral demands which are made upon them. Moral behaviour is under scrutiny and it can no longer be taken for granted that in each sphere of life the traditional codes of conduct will be obeyed. For many parents and their children there is now no generally accepted authority in ethical matters. They are confused and uncertain about standards and values. My current research into adolescent moral judgments shows that great divergences of opinion exist about the degree of rightness or wrongfulness of, for example, telling lies, sex before marriage, coveting the possessions of others, hatred and putting self first. There is increasing tolerance of variations of behaviour in all walks of life, largely due to the fact that the precise distinctions of moral codes are often blurred or toned down. The constant stress on change in every aspect of our lives – itself an expression of discontentment and perplexity – increases moral doubt, especially when at the same time people are fallaciously encouraged to trust in their own self-sufficiency. People often seem to treat one another more casually. Is the suspicion well founded that we are less considerate than previous generations? The view that 'If you don't look after yourself, no one else will', is very common among young and old alike. The apparent divorce between religion and morality is growing. So are open assaults on Christian teaching – from inside and outside the church – and on restraining rules of all kinds. On stage, screen, radio and television, orthodox attitudes are pilloried and guyed. Consequently conflict is sharpened between different codes of behaviour – home and school, home and peer groups, old and young, school and mass media, those in and those under authority.

A society in which big business, supermarkets, huge industries, great unions and even large schools are dominant, faces special moral problems. For example, those who govern and administer may become ever more remote from the governed, and the individual tends to count for less and less. Life for many people becomes more and more depersonalized. These dangers are aggravated as the pace of life and social change continues to accelerate, and as daily affairs become more complex. In such circumstances initiative is quickly blunted, and people begin to lose all sense of responsibility. Such a situation imposes particular strains on the young and inexperienced. Many of them complain bitterly of the conscious and unconscious hypocrisy of a society which preaches certain values yet does not appear to practise them in the conduct of everyday life. In fact, self-interest reigns in all walks of life, they say, and the only commandment to obey nowadays is the one that says 'thou shalt not be found out'. Problems of discipline, therefore, become especially acute. The retributive aspect of punishment is increasingly frowned upon. What is now stressed is that we impose penalties for offences to deter others from similar wrongdoing and to reform the law-breaker. The idea of personal accountability is forgotten. But punishment loses its central meaning and main justification if we do not in the first place emphasize the notion of just retribution for one's actions. Many parents are abdicating from their responsibilities by expecting the schools to instil order, manners and respect for others in their children. That's your job, not ours, they are telling teachers. Or, as a well-to-do mother recently asked the headmistress of a distinguished northern high school, 'Will you instruct my daughter to respect me?' No wonder many adolescents appear purposeless and that moral confusion abounds.

One specific reason for the current moral hesitancy amongst young and old is that a small number of eloquent speakers and writers are persistently and persuasively advocating ethical views which challenge the traditional (and usually Christian) moral standards on various issues. Those who propound these differing opinions have managed to gain much time and space on radio and television and in the press for the airing of their ideas. Thus their beliefs have been widely disseminated, and have occasioned much comment. Roughly speaking there are two main groups of people who are responsible for these attacks on the orthodox morality of our society, which until recently so many usually took for granted. The first group is composed of secularists who reject religious belief. The second is more mixed but contains a majority who do profess to be Christians and who belong to various church denominations. Let us briefly consider the main views of each group.

Of the first set of opinions, by far the most important and radical is the denial of absolute standards. According to this group, all values are relative, and no one has a right to claim that his beliefs are based on absolute truth. There is no right and wrong which is externally fixed and therefore universally valid at all times for all men everywhere, but only a better or worse, which is determined by the circumstances of the time. Acceptable views are those which appear most satisfactorily to fit the factors of man's condition and his experience at a particular time and place. My moral ideals are tentative only and should not be asserted too dogmatically because the convictions of other people may be more right than mine. I must at all times be tolerant of the sincerely held views of others. Ethical codes are still necessary, however, for the social good of man. These will usually be based, according to different secularist emphases, either on the opinions of the majority in society, or on utilitarian or prudential considerations. A third alternative favoured by some is to found moral codes upon philosophical prescriptions for which we are dependent on certain wise thinkers.

There are several serious weaknesses inherent in this position. Most of the supporters of moral relativism are genuinely concerned about man's moral betterment. Yet it is impossible for them to know whether society is making moral progress or not since they deny the absolute, objective standards which would enable them to make such an assessment. I can meaningfully argue that the moral values and practice of one group are better than those of another group *only* if the standards and conduct of both can be measured against a third impartial, true – indeed absolute – code. The ethical codes the relativists may propose, whatever their foundations, are the outcome of decisions made by fallible human beings. Also the very fact, by their own argument, that such codes have no *summum bonum* that is plainly valid for all men, always, everywhere, is a fatal weakness in their standpoint. For none of the sanctions they advocate can command the will of man absolutely. Consequently they cannot resolve the conflict between self-interest and the social good. If man is the measure of all things as they claim, why should a person put society before self? Furthermore, ethical relativism makes the tremendous and unproved assumption that all moral questions must always remain open. When challenged on these matters, the secularist attitude seems as uncertain as its answers are inconsistent.

The principal argument of the second group who have questioned orthodox thinking on morality is neatly summarized in the title of one of the Beatles' songs – 'All you need is Love'. Love is the criterion by which all actions are tested and by which all decisions to act are made. External legal codes are inadequate, even unnecessary, since love is its own law, according to many proponents in this group. Such arguments were given popular form by Bishop J. A. T. Robinson in *Honest to God.*[1] They have done much to expose the limitations of legalism and convention, but are open to counter-criticisms of poor definitions of terms. A major problem with these views is to find out exactly what is meant by 'love'. On the surface it seems that laudable Christian statements are being made, for love is the supreme mark of the Christian life. But when law and love are set in opposition, when love, and nothing else, is to determine the ethics of every situation with the result sometimes that the Biblical ethic is set aside, then serious doubts arise about the 'Christian' character of this love. So what is the relationship between law and love, according to the Bible?

C. S. Lewis has written that 'love, in the Christian sense, . . . is a state not of the feelings but of the will, that state of the will which we have naturally about ourselves and must learn to have about others'.[2] Christians know, as Paul did, that the love of Christ 'constrains' them. They must not love in word or speech, John wrote, but in deed and in truth, because love does not abrogate but fulfils the law. 'He who loves his neighbour has fulfilled the law', Paul says in Romans 13. 'Love does no wrong to a neighbour,' he adds, 'therefore love is the fulfilling of the law,' for it is the law of God that we keep his commandments. Here is an apparent paradox because the two great commandments – to love God and to love one's neighbour – are *commands* to love. 'If you love me, you will keep my commandments', said Christ at the Last

Supper, for 'if you keep my commandments, you will abide in my love'. There is another apparent paradox. The test of a Christian's love for Christ is the fact of his having and keeping Christ's commandments. In John 14 again: 'He who has my commandments and keeps them, he it is who loves me.' At the same time, the Christian's very obedience, 'keeping his words', enables him to love his Lord the more. The practical outworking of this love is seen in Christian concern for all men but especially for fellow Christians – for by the love of Christians for one another as Christ Himself stressed, 'all men will know that you are my disciples'. Christians know, as John pointed out in his first letter, that they love the children of God, 'when we love God and obey his commandments'. Christian love does not aim at self-gratification; its concern is for the needs of others. More even than this, it is as Otto Piper has noted, 'concerned with the value which the other person has in God's eyes'.[3] So Christian love, which comes from and is centred upon Christ, neither contradicts nor banishes God's law but fulfils it. Both are indispensable. John Murray's apt explanation is that 'law prescribes the action, but love it is that constrains or impels to the action involved'.[4]

Law by itself can create neither the desire nor the ability to obey it. Everything depends on the nature of the one who prescribes the regulations. Moral legalism is but cold, outward conformity. There is no real pleasure in what is commanded, nor is there real love for the lawgiver. What is not understood as clearly as it should be – and John Robinson and his friends must bear some of the blame for this – is that Christian people keep the law of their God 'not legally but evangelically', as the old Puritans used to delight to say. Christian obedience rejoices in the privilege of doing the will of God, for to carry out his wishes pleases him and benefits one's neighbour. Here is no tiresome, tedious servility but gladness of heart that one can work in harmonious fellowship with God.

But obedience does not come naturally to boys and girls, any more than it does to men and women. It has to be learned. Nevertheless the Bible offers much encouragement to spur us to carry out its precepts. There are countless examples from Abraham onwards to illustrate the truth of the assertion in Proverbs 29: 18 that the happy, blessed man is he who keeps the law. Other references in the Book of Proverbs emphasize that obedience leads to wisdom, understanding and insight. Ecclesiastes 8: 5 comments that he who obeys a command will meet no harm, thus underlining the protection that follows from adherence to the law. A lovely reference at the beginning of Proverbs 3 states that obedience also brings 'length of days and years of life and abundant welfare'. That last phrase translates the Hebrew word *shalom* which literally means 'completeness, peace'.

Of many references in the New Testament, two are particularly worth adding here. Paul reminded his Ephesian readers that it is good and right for children to obey their parents, while in 1 John 2 we read that obedience leads both to true knowledge and to increasing knowledge (verse 3), and to maturity (verse 5). Such obedience is based on love, not upon either fear or force. If commands are right and true, then one grows in loving obedience, whereas disobedience (verse 4) actually denies one the chance really to know any of these blessings.

It has been a traditional Christian claim that the revealed word of God expressly provides the directing principles for man's moral conduct. Religion and ethics have always been intimately connected, the religious imperatives providing the final authority behind the moral sanctions and also therefore the ultimate reason for man's obligation to obey. It is possible, of course, for religious ethics merely to endorse accepted patterns of behaviour, to conform, in fact, to the current moral perceptions and cultural limitations of a particular society. Christian morality, however, is not based upon the ethical speculations of men but on the revelation of God. Biblical ethics are centred not upon human aspirations, attitudes and achievements but upon the will of God for man. It is Christian morality which explains the peculiar conviction, sense, feeling, that human beings have that the main moral values are objective, not subjective. Ethics must be God-centred because true morality expresses something of the nature of God. Because man has rebelled against God, his moral thinking has been distorted. His condition is such that despite his moral consciousness and his ability independently to achieve some moral insight, he can never reliably determine from his inner moral feelings what is the will of God for himself and mankind in general. Because he is not in harmonious relationships either with his Maker or (therefore) with all his fellow human beings, he needs a frame of reference which is outside and above himself. Such an objective framework should provide definite guidance about all the main human relationships and speak clearly about man's moral duty. The law of God meets all man's requirements in these respects, speaking as it does to man's actual condition rather than to his own imagined state. It provides a corrective to man's own ethical beliefs, confirming what is worthwhile and rejecting the false or spurious. It is uncompromisingly precise on matters of principle and there is abundant historical evidence to show that obedience to its teaching promotes the health and well-being both of individual persons and of societies.

What then, according to the Bible, is the nature and purpose of the law of God? In the first place, it is divided into three parts, moral, ceremonial, and judicial, the last forming the national law of the theocratic people of Israel. Of these three, only the moral law still fully applies, since the coming of Christ abrogated the other two parts for all Christians, although some of the judicial regulations – for example, those relating to marriage and property – are still valid because they refer to institutions which remain permanently in human society. This moral law has been in existence from the beginning of time. It was not first formulated at Mount Sinai by Moses. The Ten Commandments in Exodus 20 are really a summary of the moral law, as are the two great commands to love God and one's neighbour, which Christ quoted from Deuteronomy 6 and Leviticus 19. It is worth noting in passing that the necessary relationship of the moral law with love has likewise always been there, and does not date from New Testament times as has sometimes been assumed. The law's moral norms have universal validity and application, binding the consciences of men at all times. Any breach of the law either in the letter or in the spirit, constitutes a sin against God. The commandments do not require a merely external obedience. Christ showed this plainly in his Sermon on the Mount. They are spiritual and reach down to man's inmost thoughts and disposition. The law is holy, just and good. Its injunctions and prohibitions are perfectly sensible, reasonable and fair. They are all calculated to promote the highest good of all men. There is not one which is not excellent or which does not commend itself to men's consciences and to their good judgment. They do not attempt to prescribe regulations which take care of every possibility in life. Nevertheless in proclaiming certain basic principles, the moral law offers a timeless statement of behaviour which God requires of all reasonable persons in their thoughts, words and deeds.

In the second place, the purpose of the law of God, according to the Bible, is at least fivefold. Its primary function is didactic, giving accurate information about the character of God and of the code of conduct that he demands of mankind. The law is not merely a series of abstract rules to which conformity is required, but it has been given as a means to know God and his will for his creation. For one of the main truths that it emphasizes is that whether men accept the fact or not there is a relationship between man and God which is both personal and permanent. The second and third functions of the law concern sin. Objectively the law shows up sin in its true colours. It is only by means of the moral law that sin is seen to be the evil thing it is. Also, because the law proclaims the will of God, it helps to restrain sin and preserve order in the world. Subjectively, one of the purposes of the law is to awaken and deepen the conviction of sin in the consciences of both individuals and nations. Yet the law aims at more than conviction. In the fourth place it brings man, now conscious of his own failures, to Christ the Saviour, whose earthly life provides the perfect example of complete obedience to the moral law. The law exposes a man's moral imperfection and guilt, thereby uncovering his need for redemption which only Christ can accomplish. Finally, the fifth function of the law is normative, providing a rule for Christian behaviour, a rule by which Christians can order their lives, and a criterion of what is morally good and virtuous. As well as offering comprehensive moral principles, there are particular rules which relate to certain aspects of daily life. And as John Murray's comment already quoted reminds us, Christian love provides the impetus which leads to personal obedience and to the service of others.

Christian morality is not just a series of 'thou shalt nots', nor is Christian obedience an arbitrary and legalistic following out of certain Scriptural injunctions. The negative aspects of conduct are stressed. But then so are the positive sanctions. True obedience to the law of God is always a positive and constructive response. It is never the mechanical observance of an abstract set of moral rules. In the Christian life, under the 'new covenant', it is love and thankfulness which chiefly motivate the believer in his keeping of the law. At the centre of Christian morality is dependence on God. It is the judgment of God, not the individual conscience, that provides the final standard. For the Christian the cardinal issue is not goodness, but holiness, purity, 'the state of mind produced when the soul is full of God', as Charles Hodge magnificently defined it.[5] 'Be holy, for I am holy' is the often repeated Scriptural maxim. The root meaning of the term 'holy' is 'separate, cut off from all profane use and content'. The godly man, in Biblical terms, is not so much the moral man as the man who is separated, saved, from evil. Nevertheless, evidence of his set-apart condition is seen in the righteous, obedient life he tries to lead. This life demonstrates the most glorious part of Christian morality. For the will of God is not some distant, external set of rules to which we must conform. God is at the centre of successful Christian living, effectually energizing and creating in his people the power and the desire to will and work for his satisfaction and delight.

There remains the crucial problem of the moral education of children and young people. Because of the confusion concerning ethical issues today and also because there is a greater understanding about the moral development of the young, the demand grows louder for more moral teaching both in and out of school. The Biblical emphasis undoubtedly supports this demand. It underlines the importance of the direct moral education of children, a task for which parents are primarily but not solely responsible. This education must take account of both positive and negative considerations. The consequences of disobedience should be outlined as clearly as the positive rewards which come from faithful adherence to the law of God. In all this, Biblical instruction is concerned not merely with the external penalties and accolades which moral conduct merits. It is the effects on individual character and personal relationships which its teaching most strongly emphasizes. So, in the words of Ecclesiastes 7: 5, 'it is better for a man to hear the rebuke of the wise than to hear the song of fools'. The Book of Proverbs not only praises wisdom, outlines the blessings which follow from obedience to the law and to parental counsel, and extols the virtuous woman; it also issues strong warnings against such dangers as sexual sins, the evils of the tongue, self-indulgence and the loss of self-control generally. Indirect moral education is not enough. Both the Old Testament and the New reveal that private conduct has social repercussions and that we are all intimately bound up with one another. Consequently the training of character is the most vital part of any child's upbringing.

In any case, the development of moral awareness is more essential for individual and social health than the development of intellect or of physical fitness. For when a nation's moral sense is blunted, so its social life and structure degenerate. As Peter reminded his readers, quoting from Psalm 34, 'he who would love life and see good days . . . let him turn away from evil and do right'. History has repeatedly shown that moral health is crucial to a country's success in all its activities. The fall of many great nations has been hastened, and often set in motion in the first place, by growing moral degeneracy. Biblical teaching repeatedly claims to offer the wholesome preservative needed by all peoples. As Isaiah 26: 9 asserts in its praise of God, 'when thy judgments are in the earth, the inhabitants of the world learn righteousness'. The word 'learn' translates the Hebrew word *lamad*. As noted in the first chapter, this word has the idea of self-control according to a given standard. It also denotes the idea of acquiring understanding and the idea of accustoming oneself to something, in this case 'righteousness'. Consequently the Bible is claiming that when God's precepts are taught and practised, everybody benefits.

As far as a child's formal education is concerned, at school he is a member of a community, many of the ties and demands of which are moral. It is one of the tasks of every school to assist in the personal development of its pupils, and to help them increasingly to understand what is involved in responsible living. As was implied earlier in the chapter, it is important to educate consciences so that individual and collective thinking, judging and acting might be more in accord with right standards. So if Biblical teaching about man's nature, needs and duties is to be heeded, the schools should play a definite part in assisting their pupils' moral development.

This cannot be allowed to proceed haphazardly. Research has shown that a majority of teachers in maintained schools in England and Wales support the introduction of direct moral education lessons into school timetables, especially at the secondary level.[6] In a further piece of research, over 71 per cent of a nationwide random sample of 14–16 year-olds have also indicated their desire to have special periods for moral education.[6] Such periods could reinforce the indirect moral training that goes on in school more or less all the time. The moral awareness of children is helped through a balanced curriculum and through the study of individual subjects – literature, history and religious knowledge being the most obvious of these. Much moral guidance comes through the exercise of discipline, especially if this is done wisely and with sympathy both in the individual case and in communal problems. Under common grace we can confidently look to the schools to give some effective training both in the concept of law and in obedience to law.

Giving pupils some responsibility helps to teach them self-reliance and to respect the needs and wishes of others. Community living can greatly encourage moral growth, especially if group values are right and the pupils can gain experience through the practice of the precepts advocated. The ethos of a school has a crucial influence on the moral education of its pupils. Much harm may be done if the actual values of a school conflict with its publicly stated aims. The goals set before pupils, the standards implicit in all activities, the values openly emphasized, all contribute to the 'tone' of a school, and help to form pupils' moral judgments. In particular, the way in which rules are applied, and the personal example of the teachers and the older pupils, all play a vital part in influencing children's moral awareness. If young people are ever to be helped to make their own responsible moral choices, then the characteristic community spirit of a school must clearly reflect high standards and real compassion and respect for others. Christian teaching and vision obviously have a significant contribution to make here.

But as so many Biblical writers have stressed, definite, explicit guidance in moral issues is also essential. In this respect a very varied programme is possible given the time and support of the teaching staff. Individual and group discussions, analysis of social problems and case studies, training in the exercise of moral judgment, some elementary study of moral codes and of the law of the land, assisting pupils to consider and reconsider such codes in the light of practical experience, these are some of the activities which might contribute to a moral education syllabus. Yet most Christians would affirm that at the heart of all moral teaching of the young, wherever this is undertaken, there should be Scriptural precepts. All children should be taught to know about and understand Christian moral principles. At the very least they will then be in a position to accept or reject them knowingly and with recognition of the consequences of their choice. For Biblical ethical teaching covers every important social relationship – that between husband and wife, parents and children, employer and employee, citizens and the state, the individual and his neighbour, nation and nation, Christian and non-Christian. And over and above all these it emphasizes the relationship between man and God. It takes the only fully realistic view of man and all his deepest problems. All the main aspects of man's moral situation are considered. Christian morality provides a positive, objective standard against which all human actions may be measured. Against this framework children and adults alike can test their presuppositions and their actions, and can find support to uphold them in periods of difficulty and confusion. Here is the truly authoritative guide at all times. For Christian ethics have the ultimate authority which is lacking in every man-made speculative ethical system. This authority both undergirds and explains man's obligation to obey.

It is worth insisting that here is no mere advocacy of a return to an old, unthinking, 'because the Bible says so' approach. We must attend with all our mind to Biblical teaching because its description of human life and human relationships is accurate. Life *is* like this. The word of God *fits* ourselves in the world as we find it. It also fits us as we find ourselves. The simplest and best way to prove this is to borrow from the classroom the modern method of learning by discovery. If children are sent out to investigate the world around them, and especially the world of personal relationships, they will quickly find for themselves how appropriate is the Biblical description of man and of man in society. They will discover that only the Christian world picture can accommodate and explain *all* the data. No other world view acknowledges and accounts for all the evidence. No other teaching provides such comprehensive and practical guidance to help us meet the demands of each new day.

No aspect of our life is morally neutral or, Christians would add, outside the sphere of God's command. The Scriptural ideal is that all relationships are to be governed by Christian love and all acts by Biblical principles. It is therefore essential to teach children what this means and what it involves for them personally and socially. It is equally essential that Christian moral principles permeate the whole education service, guiding educational thinking and practice at every level. Their influence will, however, only be felt with force if Christians in education, as everywhere else, proclaim them, apply them, and in their own lives exemplify them. For in the end if men are truly to live, they must obey the law of God and walk in his way. Man is so created that to choose the alternative is fatal.

REFERENCES TO CHAPTER NINE

1 J. A. T. Robinson, *Honest to God*, SCM Press, 1963.
2 C. S. Lewis, *Mere Christianity*, Fontana Books, 1955, p. 113.
3 Otto A. Piper, *Christian Ethics*, Nelson, 1970, p. 175.
4 John Murray, *Principles of Conduct*, Tyndale Press, 1957, p. 22.
5 Charles Hodge, *Systematic Theology*, Vol. II, James Clarke, 1960, p. 101.
6 See P. R. May, *Moral Education in School*, Methuen Educational Ltd., 1971, for a detailed study of the whole subject. In addition to an extensive account of the research into teachers' attitudes, there is a chapter on adolescent attitudes to moral education in which details of the research project among 14 – 16 year-olds are given.

Chapter Ten
THE CHRISTIAN TEACHER

Any Christian, whatever his occupation, faces his daily tasks from a very advantageous position. He knows that his God is the one, true, sovereign Lord of all, who has revealed himself and his will for man. This gracious self-disclosure has been effected through Christ, through Scripture and through the whole of creation. The knowledge affords him a securely based view of himself and his world. He knows that all life is sacred, and that it has rational meaning and definite purpose. There is a goal at which to aim, the glorifying of God, and this should influence everything he does. He knows that all history, past, present and future, is under God's control. Every event serves to further God's plan for all mankind. There is mystery here which the Christian cannot explain, but that does not frighten him. His knowledge of the character of God in Christ engenders assurance and comfort even in the face of incomplete understanding. Because he cannot see the whole picture he is unable fully to grasp even his own contribution. Yet it is possible for him to play his part with complete trust. For he also knows that the providence of God is at work, while this present age lasts, for the benefit of all mankind, and especially for the good of the church and every individual believer.

Consequently the Christian rests in, and speaks and acts from, a secure vantage-point, although this fact offers him no cause for self-congratulation. Christians must beware of complacency or smugness, but this is no reason for any watering down of the confidence and assurance with which the New Testament rings. What a contrast with so many others, at the heart of whose thought and practice is muddle and insecurity concerning man's world and destiny. Finite man is incapable of comprehending the whole truth about God and life, but Christianity has wholeness and consistency of thought, and does answer the most fundamental questions. About certain truths the Christian can speak with absolute assurance. He knows, for instance, that God created the universe, though he cannot say when or how this was done; he knows that Jesus Christ, the Son of God, died for him on the cross, rose again from the dead and gives new life to all who put their trust in him. About certain mysteries he can without any qualms admit that he does not know the answers. He believes that one day Christ will come again to judge the living and the dead and that 'a new heaven and a new earth' will replace the existing ones. Yet how or when this will happen he cannot tell. Despite this ignorance, all is well. One way of describing this situation is to say that the Christian is aware of his own limitations as a creature. He accepts these restrictions and enjoys a freedom of enquiry *determined by* this awareness. He can live successfully and happily with certain questions unanswered. For he trusts the God he knows. The Christian is commanded to be *in* the world but not *of* it. He must strive therefore to comprehend his present situation as fully as possible, even though he recognizes that his knowledge will be partial. Such understanding principally depends upon his grasp of the process of history and his insight into man's relationships with his fellows. History is not a chance affair which began who knows how and which will end who knows when. It is the positive out-working of the will of God, from its foreordained start to its predetermined conclusion, the key to the whole being Christ. As Biblical teaching from Genesis to Revelation explain this, so it is from Scripture that the Christian can gain the perception he needs about the nature and demands of personal relationships. He can recognize the problems brought about by the disrupting effects of sin. He is also given positive moral and social guidance to help him to realize both his own obligations in behaviour to others and the principles of right conduct in general.

The Christian must work to apply the revealed will of God in his particular situation. By witnessing to the truth and trying to maintain it, in other words by shouldering his Christian responsibilities, he is helping to further God's purpose for human society. He must help to maintain (or create) stability in his situation by upholding order and opposing confusion. For the Christian teacher, this means, among other things, maintaining discipline. To allow pupils to run riot, even in the name of free discovery methods, or to be inconsistent in the treatment (and especially the punishment) of individuals, will hardly foster that respect for others and control of self which are central to good order and discipline. Wherever possible the Christian should try to influence social thinking and action according to Christian principles. For the teacher this will mean that from time to time he will actively assist his colleagues and the parents of his pupils to recognize a Christian point of view, where such exists, on educational issues. He will support God's basic outline for society by helping to ensure that no one main sphere of authority – whether the family, the church or the state – encroaches upon or usurps the right of another.

For example, the teacher, as the state's appointed servant, should not trespass deliberately on rights which properly belong to the parents. Teachers certainly have a definite job to do *in loco parentis* but this does not entitle them to assume that the education of children is a task in which parents should play no effective part. Schools which, in the past, have prevented parents from having any say about the courses their children should take, or which have neglected to consult parents when giving pupils careers guidance or instruction in personal matters such as sex education, have been guilty of such wrongful intrusion. The point is not that such teaching is not to be given in school but that it should not be given without the full knowledge, consent and co-operation of the home. On the other hand, teachers should not be expected automatically to take over certain duties simply because many parents are failing to do these things properly at home.

Religious education, teaching about sex and marriage and providing meals for pupils are just three examples of family responsibilities which some parents want the schools largely, if not entirely, to carry out for them. There are also sound educational arguments justifying all three activities in school, and in any case few teachers would deny children help in these matters at school if they knew their pupils were starved of them at home. Yet in undertaking such duties, the schools should continue to make clear to parents that theirs, not the teachers, is the prime responsibility for all these tasks.

The Christian should, as far as he can, help to enrich the culture of his society against the corruption of sin, and use every chance he has to do good to others. He must, in short, *be* a Christian, giving thanks for all the blessings which God liberally showers upon his creation. Finally, the Christian should always bear in mind what Harry Blamires calls 'eternal perspectives'. He must 'mentally inhabit a world with a Heaven above it and a Hell beneath it, a world in which man is called to live daily, hourly, in contact with the God whom neither time nor space can limit'.[1] These perspectives provide a corrective against becoming too fully immersed in the affairs of everyday life. For this age will not last for ever. It is not permanent. Nor will utopia ever be realized in this age. The perfect life is still to come, when the present 'heaven and earth' have passed away.

These general considerations are particularly relevant to the Christian in the teaching situation. As one who is to guide and instruct children in the way they should go, the Christian teacher should be quite clear about the nature and responsibilities of his role. He has a distinctive contribution to make and not only by *being* a Christian. He must also apply Biblical thinking to his own practice as a teacher and to educational discussion generally. This is all part of the Christian's duty to be both 'salt' and 'light' wherever he finds himself. What, then, of the office of teacher, so highly regarded in Scripture? A number of factors should be recognized.

In the first place, every teacher stands before his pupils not only as a representative of wisdom and knowledge but as a representative of truth. In the eyes of his pupils and of society, he is a man of specialist knowledge and understanding. Part of the authority of his office stems from this fact. As regards the content of his lessons, he knows what his classes need to learn. They are dependent on him and look to him for help with those areas of his learning that *he* decides they need to master. Although he will frequently point his classes beyond himself, for much of their school lives *he* is the authority for them in his particular field. They will accept his word, his information, his judgment. All this is true whether the method he happens to be using is one of direct instruction, or whether he is encouraging his pupils to find out knowledge and gain experience for themselves in an environment that he has structured for them. Obviously in practice there are individual exceptions, due in most cases to the personalities of both teacher and pupils concerned. Where such differences occur it is the responsibility of the whole school, and if necessary of the local authority and the parents, to ensure that the authority of the teacher is acknowledged and respected. It is not simply a matter for the persons immediately concerned. This is because teaching is a team task and schools are living communities, not a series of isolated class units. If those directly involved can settle the issues themselves, so much the better. Yet individual teachers may well need all-round support as they learn to master their job. Pupils, the rebellious ones most of all, require firmness and sympathetic help to understand the considerate part they must play if relationships are to be successful and progress is to be achieved. Perhaps today there is also an exception subject-wise, for religious education teachers often have to battle with ignorant prejudice and scepticism before they can begin to succeed. Usually, however, the prevailing view is that what teacher says, is right.

The teacher needs, therefore, to be a master of his subject and also to see it in a wider perspective, relating it wherever possible to the other aspects of the curriculum. He should not teach his subject in isolation from the rest. The history of ideas – such as the notion of progress or of evolution – demonstrates the interdependence of many subjects at particular points. To understand parts of the poetry of Donne and Milton for example, demands knowledge of the history of astronomy and of seventeenth-century scientific ideas, so many of which were in fact popularized and made acceptable through this poetry and the writings of other non-scientists such as Francis Bacon. No teacher should encourage the building round his subject of barriers which the often arbitrary divisions of the school timetable will in any case suggest. There are indeed distinct fields of knowledge. But truths in each area are not always unrelated and pupils need to be made aware of relationships where they exist. Christians would add that since God is the source of all truth, those who teach should consider their field of study with this fact in mind.

The one position that no one can adopt who is involved in education in any way and at any level, is that of neutrality. Some confusion exists at the present time about this. For to be clear and definite in one's views is to court disapproval from some quarters and risks the charges of dogmatism and being authoritarian, especially if one is a teacher of the young. There is currently much talk about encouraging young people to make up their own minds on all the issues of life that confront them. Pupils should not be told what to think. One might infer from some arguments that they should not be told anything at all but left to discover for themselves. One aim of school life, according to many voices, is to bring the young to positions where they can make their own decisions. Alternatively, the groundwork for future decision-making should be laid. In other words, all teaching should be as objective as possible at least to the extent that, where different views exist, pupils will be helped to understand as far as they can the factors and implications of each standpoint. Certain history, social studies, general science and religious education lessons are obvious cases at issue when varying ideas will need to be considered.

There is much to commend in these arguments. Yet there remains every good teacher's commitment to his subject and to his job, and the need always to teach with conviction and enthusiasm. One cannot be neutral either about one's pupils or about what one teaches. We are all either for or against one basic belief or another, even though we may not have worked out our own particular philosophic position. Fence-sitting is impossible for any human being where ultimate convictions are concerned, whatever some people may like to imagine to the contrary. And we carry our fundamental beliefs with us wherever we go, in school and out. They colour our teaching, our relationships, everything. It is still possible, indeed it is essential in all one's dealings with young people, to be fair in helping them towards their own responsible decision-making at various levels. Care must be taken not to pressurize pupils to favour one's own ideas. Yet one does not have to adopt a pretence of neutrality. It is the teachers with real convictions who usually command the greatest respect among young people.

As a representative of truth, the teacher bears some responsibility towards the whole truth in the situation in which he finds himself. He ought not to shy away from this fact. Just as with discipline and the running of the school he is one of a team and his approach, his success, or his failure, will have repercussions on his colleagues, so in the presentation of his particular subject he must recognize that what he says and what he teaches will influence attitudes towards, and understanding of, truth in general. In all this he has two main tasks as a teacher. The first is to make truth known, as clearly and effectively as he can. The second is to show his pupils how they should respond to truth. For all to whom truth is communicated immediately have some responsibility towards that truth, a responsibility to grasp it, master it, commit themselves to it. It is the teacher's task, as a representative of truth, to make his pupils clearly aware of their accountability in this matter.

Closely linked to this point is the need to impress upon pupils of all ages the crucial importance of truth-telling. For truthfulness is one of the key virtues of youth. It is a habit that needs to be acquired as early as possible, for honest dealings are central to every successful human relationship throughout life. Yet the temptation to tell lies is one to which children are especially vulnerable. The seriousness of this practice – according to Christ it is characteristic of Satan himself – should never be disguised from children under such euphemisms as 'fibs' or 'white lies' or 'telling stories'. Indeed because lying is so spiritually harmful and so often practised with deliberate calculation, it should be punished much more severely than other common sins of childhood like selfishness or greed.

Another factor concerning the Christian teacher is that he needs to test his ideas and practice wherever possible against the revealed word of God. It is worth repeating again that to argue thus is not to imply that the Bible is a complete pedagogical primer for teachers. Yet, as this book has tried to demonstrate, throughout Scripture there is much of relevance to education at all levels. The Scriptures present a view of God, mankind and the universe which provides a perspective for teaching as for the whole of life. Christian teaching contributes to the study of the nature of education and educational processes and also to the quality of education. The Christian teacher therefore needs to work out for himself the Biblical world view and relate it to his work. St Augustine, as George Howie has pointed out, devoted part of his *De Doctrina Christiana* to 'the proposition that the teacher who is not committed to a philosophy of life can neither find his own direction nor give direction to others, no matter how polished or lucid his style of delivery or how cultivated his manner'.[2] Technical ability alone is not enough. Stephen Bayne makes a further point which is pertinent here. He argues that because Christianity became the source and ground of European civilization, 'the teacher of science, or poetry, or law, or history, has a greater responsibility for the understanding of the Christian contribution to Western society than the teacher of religion *per se* could ever have'.[3] The teacher will be better able, therefore, to fulfil his responsibilities, once he has gained the insights and the world view which the Bible provides for him. He will be much more able to take sides responsibly in educational controversies, recognizing what his position is in the light of Biblical doctrine. He will not simply float aimlessly along from one attitude to the next.

The teacher is accountable to God for his teaching and handling of the truth. This should mean that he recognizes his need for humility before God, a humility which he should take with him into all his work. The Christian knows that he is dependent on God in all things and that his gifts are God-given. Humility itself demands that he should develop these God-given talents to the full, so that as a teacher he may present truth rightly, effectively, and with boldness. What kind of boldness is proper to a Christian in this respect? Some people regard any kind of prohibition in study as an unfair exercise of authority, for they desire uninhibited enquiry and discussion. But the Christian is aware that there are limits to research and enquiry; notably there are limits to the effectiveness of speculation about the future and about the supernatural. Likewise there may be certain perhaps sordid, lewd or shocking aspects of a particular subject which it would be neither helpful nor proper to discuss with pupils. In such instances the teacher may well be right to exercise censorship out of respect for the children and young people in his charge as well as for the Lord to whom he is answerable for all things. Here again, accountability to God underlines not only the importance of that positive virtue of humility, but also the responsibility of the office of teacher. Teaching is a privileged work which should not be undertaken lightly.

A further consideration with regard to the office of teacher concerns his judicial authority. Although the effective exercise of rule and of justice depends very considerably upon the character and personality of the teacher, authority does not inhere in his person. The Christian knows that the character and authority of God and his revealed will provide both the basis and the example for all proper human authority. The teacher's role as one who imparts knowledge and skills, and one who must guide and control children and young people, carries with it power to command, lead and adjudicate. How he uses this power will largely determine how much respect, obedience and affection are shown by his pupils both to his office and to his own person. As the employee and representative of the state, or the governing body, he represents the law. Consequently it is a crucial part of his office to uphold and administer law, a task he must try to perform with wisdom, justice and mercy. As every teacher knows, one must not only be fair, but be seen by one's pupils to be fair. The need to love one's neighbour is especially pressing here. There will be tensions between such love and the duty of carrying out the judicial functions which all teachers are called upon from time to time to exercise. Such tensions often arise from the fact that it is not easy for children to understand that insistence on obedience to the rules of the school community, and any punishment they may receive for wrong-doing are – or should be if the teacher-pupil relationship is a right one – an expression of loving concern as well as of justice. It is never easy to be unprejudiced in these matters. Yet a teacher is more likely to be impartial if he genuinely cares for his pupils. The Christian model is the approach of God himself who 'disciplines him whom he loves and chastises every son whom he receives'.

Punishment should be seen primarily to be just retribution for the offence committed, for this is its essence. Any reforming or deterrent effects are always secondary. Likewise in a consistent environment rewards should be given for meritorious achievement in work or conduct rather than as spurs to such ends. One sometimes hears it said that to withhold punishment, especially corporal punishment, helps a child to understand what love and forgiveness mean. Such talk is almost always an expression not of love but of sentimentality, and the advice it offers should be followed only on exceptional occasions. For younger children the short sharp slap and the occasional spanking can be far more effective means of communicating the just deserts for wrong-doing than any attempt to reason with the offender, who is usually impervious to logical argument anyway. But some people allege that what Louis Arnaud Reid once described as 'bodily personal communication of authoritative indignant moral condemnation'[4] has no morally good result at all. At best it causes children to avoid wrong-doing out of fear. Even to say 'No' might cause repressions which will have harmful effects when the child is older. Such objections have force only if the relation between teacher and pupil (or parent and child) is one of harsh negativism. In a normal, healthy relationship wrongdoing rarely figures prominently and such punishment as is necessary is seen by everyone against a background of care, concern and sympathetic understanding. Punishment, if fair and properly delivered, makes all who are involved aware that there is a moral authority above us all, and laws which we break at our peril. It actually reinforces the moral ties between teachers and pupils.

Last, but by no means least, every teacher acts to a greater or lesser extent *in loco parentis*. Although there is nothing in statutory law about this, the teacher's role as 'parent' is unavoidable. It will vary according to the type of school in which he teaches, the age of his pupils, and the area in which the school and the homes of the children are situated. Also the opportunities to exercise parental roles will vary. Nevertheless parents entrust their children each day into the care of the schools, and therefore whilst the children are in their care the head teachers and their staff have to fulfil certain parental responsibilities. At the very least these will include right teaching, sound discipline and real love and concern for children, all duties which the Bible lays in the first place at the door of the parents. As is his judicial function, so also the teacher's parental authority is delegated to him. Above all as a 'parent' he represents love. Thus it matters vitally what kind of a person he is. As a representative of law, he must be impartial, and in this respect at least his character as an individual should not enter into the situation. As the representative of love, however, his own characteristics as a person are all-important in determining how he will fulfil this aspect of the teaching office. He will certainly not like every child he teaches, but it is his duty to love each one of them. This is a matter not so much of establishing warm, intimate relationships with his pupils, although kindness and sympathy must characterize his approach. Rather is it actively to will for every one of them all that is good, true and wholesome.

In chapter seven it was remarked that parents should give their children security and protection as part of their task of providing for the young. For the home is a place of refuge as well as a centre of joy and a harbourage from which to journey forth. The school, especially for younger children, has a similar function, and part of the teacher's role is to be a shield for his pupils. The aim is not to produce hot-house flowers which wilt the moment they feel the cold, but to provide normal, healthy growth. This means that teachers, like parents, will need to protect their pupils from all that may harm or stunt their growth. The classroom, like the home, should be a base where young people can find help with their problems, shelter from worldly pressures which would have them grow up too quickly in conformity with the images of passing fashion, safety from disorder and confusion particularly in behaviour and standards, protection sometimes even from the folly or unwisdom of their own immature, ill-founded judgments and feelings, and from their own self-will and the unkindness of their playmates and friends.

Above all things children need to be protected as far as possible from evil in all its forms. Coarseness, brutality, cruelty, blasphemy, foul language, sarcasm, the prurient and pornographic, evil talk, flagrant immodesty of all kinds, all of which abound today, harden the heart and damage the spirit of man. They invariably emanate from sceptical, scornful, twisted minds from whom real respect for persons, real love of neighbour is wholly absent. The teaching environment should be free of such elements. Scepticism itself should be shunned at all costs, for this is a less obvious, more insidious evil. It can quickly destroy childish innocence with all its readiness to trust. Open-minded we certainly want our pupils to be as they approach different subjects. But the spirit of doubting breeds a withered heart. Scepticism is no mark of moral or intellectual superiority as some academics would have us believe. It is thoroughly negative, a stumbling-block to all loving relationships and the intimate understanding of anything. Teachers, like parents, must give good things to their children and young people.

These last comments raise the whole question of the teacher's character. What sort of person should become a teacher? F. E. Gaebelein has listed five main qualifications for the Christian teacher. He should be a Christian, be intellectually able, be a wholesome personality – balance, humour, patience, self-control, firmness, endurance and common sense are qualities which Gaebelein suggests contribute to this – he should have love for young people, and have a call to teach.[5] Some of the most important things in education are passed on by example rather than precept. And pupils invariably catch something of the minds, manners and ways of their teachers. In previous chapters it has been implied that character development is the most important part of any person's upbringing and that therefore while recognizing the importance of intelligence in moral development, moral training is to be pursued more urgently than development of intellect. This also affects the teacher. It means that what the teacher *is* matters more than how well-qualified he happens to be, even though excellent academic standards are most desirable in all schoolmasters and schoolmistresses no matter what the age group with which they are concerned. It means also that what the teacher *is* matters more than what he teaches. For it is generally true, whether one is teaching infants, primary or secondary school children, students or adults, that one's teaching is accepted as one is oneself accepted. Also, as mature and responsible adults, head teachers and their colleagues provide valuable models for their pupils. And for some children they may be the only examples of real care and patience that they experience. They certainly represent for most pupils the most significant images of the adult world, outside their immediate family, with whom they come in close, regular contact.

Two important conclusions follow from these two facts. The teacher, firstly, needs to be a committed person. Christians would say, 'committed to Christ', not because they think that Christian teachers are the best, but because commitment to Christ radically changes one's nature and one's awareness of the purpose of life and the true needs of man. Furthermore, as W. R. Niblett has pointed out, 'there is nothing irrational about commitment; it is permanent non-commitment that seeks to trade out of human life and the nature of things.'[6] The second conclusion is aptly summarized in Martin Buber's often-quoted dictum that the teacher must himself be what he wants his pupils to become. Christianity underlines the fact that the perfect standard for both teachers and pupils alike is Christ. When children realize this, it makes their own education more meaningful. Their experience and their understanding of life are harmonized when they come to see that they are being encouraged to travel the same road, according to the same rules, that their parents and teachers are travelling, with the example of Christ as the objective of it all.

Teaching is not an easy occupation. It is stimulating, has many rewards and satisfactions, and is vitally important in any society. It is also demanding, involving much hard work and some self-sacrifice. Professional competence demands much study and practice as well as imagination, flexibility, insight into the nature and needs of the young, and good health. Patience is an especially necessary quality not merely because of the constant demands made every day upon the teacher's time and energies. With many children, the desired results of one's efforts are not seen quickly, and sometimes not at all, even when an impression has been made. Likewise honesty. Children quickly discern whom they can trust. The teacher who wants respect for himself and his office must be patently honest. This includes readiness to admit when he is ignorant or mistaken. Such courage will immeasurably strengthen his authority in the eyes of his pupils. Paul's advice to the Galatians not to be weary in well-doing, 'for in due season we shall reap', applies readily to the school situation. The teacher's task is a most significant one. He is not just concerned to pass on certain basic skills and knowledge, and to create opportunities for children to learn. He is dealing with human souls, and whatever his specialist subject may be (if he has one), he is contributing in one way or another to the spiritual, moral, mental and physical development of all the pupils in his charge. One particular problem, from the Christian standpoint, which the teacher shares with others outside school, is that of helping children to grow up out of their weak, childish ways and be prepared for entry into the adult world, yet all the while assisting them to retain those aspects of childhood which are pre-requisites for entry into the kingdom of God. It is not easy for the young to realize that ready obedience is the way both to maturity and to 'meekness', strength-with-humility.

What, then, should be the Christian's approach to the job of teaching? A Christian perspective can and should determine both attitudes and action. Like all who enter the teaching profession, the Christian teacher should be properly, professionally equipped. He should be master of his subject-matter and flexible in methods of teaching, being ready to examine and try out new ideas. He should be clear about his educational objectives and must strive to keep up to date in his understanding of child development. He must work out the scope and limitations of his particular post from a Christian viewpoint and apply Christian wholeness in the context in which he is placed. If he chooses, as most do, to work in a secular context – and what he is as a person ought to come out in his application for the post and at interview – he must accept the framework in which he finds himself, just as the head teacher and appointing authority must accept him as he is once he is appointed.

In fulfilling efficiently all the legitimate demands of the job, the Christian teacher must show forth Christ. His Christian values will be constantly under pressure and challenge. They should be manifest not only in his attitude to his work and his pupils, in his discipline and in his stewardship of time, but also in his personal standards, in his staffroom conduct and in all his professional activities. All he does should be characterized by integrity and consistency both in and out of school. His treatment of others should be full of loving concern, defending their rights, considering their needs and honestly respecting their views and expertise. He should be willing to learn from his colleagues and his pupils as well as to give what he can from his own experience and wisdom. And in all things he must stand firm. What considerable demands all this makes upon him! Yet he does not stand alone. He knows this as a Christian; he should always remember it as a teacher. He should be concerned to promote the all-round development of all his pupils, but his is not the sole reponsibility for this – a fact which young, enthusiastic, caring teachers occasionally forget. He has a vital job, but it is a team task that he has entered into.

Many teachers today would say that the main part of their task is concerned with the pastoral care of their pupils. Their role *in loco parentis* underlines this. As one Christian headmaster has written, pastoral care 'is actively desiring the good of the children in our charge'. He goes on to point out that it is 'not a voluntary extra in teaching', but 'a fundamental attitude of mind within the classroom that sees each child as an individual, distinct from all the other children in the group'.[7] The teacher's role has come much more under scrutiny in recent days and arguments may now sometimes be heard about certain aspects of the duties of a head and his staff. The problems of pastoral care are among those which figure in current discussions. John Hansford feels that nowadays there is not a great deal of dispute about what pastoral care ought to involve. He says: 'The difficulty is to find the power to put it into practice and to keep it from a steady deterioration; it is at this stage that the relevance of the Christian gospel becomes apparent.'[8] For Christianity is concerned about *every* individual, and directs us to the source of power by which to care for them.

Scriptural insights into the nature and needs of children, and recommendations concerning the content of education are revealing and helpful, especially to the inexperienced teacher. Any young Christian who is thinking of entering the teaching profession will find much to guide him, in both the Old and the New Testaments. Many examples have already been quoted in this book. Paul's letters to Timothy, although containing advice applicable to any Christian whatever his job, are particularly relevant to the young student or new teacher, not least because Timothy himself was young and inexperienced when he received these communications from Paul. He should take heed to himself and his teaching. He should keep himself pure, letting none despise his youth but set an example in speech, conduct, love, faith and purity. His attitude to his work is also important. He must not neglect his gifts but exercise them, and be diligent, as professionally efficient and effective as possible, a workman who has no need to be ashamed. He must not get *too* involved in this world's affairs so that he loses sight of the main purpose of life. It is possible to become so immersed in the work and problems of a school that these demands become the be-all and end-all of life. In such a situation it is difficult to be objective and to see matters in proper perspective. In his attitude to others and to authority he should be respectful, kindly and forbearing, avoiding senseless controversies and idle gossip. How easy it is to grumble about or to resent conditions of work, or the methods of the head teacher, or certain colleagues, or particular classes or pupils. Lastly, concerning his working conditions, there is great gain in 'godliness with contentment', especially since the Christian knows that Christ has appointed him to his service, and will keep him to the end. This does not mean that no Christian teacher should ever seek promotion, or to better his circumstances in his job. The best conditions are essential for the sake of the pupils as well as the staff, though whether or not one should go on strike to obtain them is a matter for each individual conscience. The phrase 'godliness with contentment' really describes a consistent attitude of unself-seeking meekness, patience and temperance, those positive traits which combine with thankfulness as characteristic marks of a godly person. Christ himself provides the supreme example of the ideal teacher. He came to give life and to give it more abundantly. Therefore the Christian should be, above all, the advocate, the expositor and the exemplar of the abundant life.

All teachers face certain problems, wherever they teach. There are the dangers of getting into a rut, and becoming resistant to new ideas and approaches. There is the problem of keeping up to date with one's subject. The temptation comes to many, especially the unmarried, to limit one's whole life to one's school, and never cultivate any outside friends and interests. It is very hard sometimes to be sympathetic and fair to those pupils who have little aptitude for or interest in one's own subject, or with whom it is not easy to be friendly. And what about those days when one is off colour, when staff absences mean extra work, when one's pupils seem particularly perverse or uninterested, when the daily round is especially wearying? These are real tests of personality, when the need just to persevere and go on caring are greatest. But some problems may press upon the Christian teacher particularly. He may undertake too many Christian activities. It is not given to many people to be able to run a youth club, attend regular midweek meetings, teach in the Sunday school and still be a fresh and fully effective schoolmaster or schoolmistress, especially in the early stages of one's teaching career. Some young Christians may tend to regard their subject and their daily work as secondary and inferior to their church work. Frequently linked to this attitude is the failure to think Christianly about anything other than religious matters. It is very easy to leave education or science or politics or commerce to the current experts in these fields and to try to apply Christian principles only to church activities. This is to suggest that these principles have no general reference at all, when the Biblical approach is to stress their importance over the whole of life. Christian neglect of these issues quickly leads one to the unconscious acceptance of standards which may be sub-

Christian. Alternatively the over-zealous Christian teacher may see his work as a heaven-sent opportunity for daily evangelism, in which he takes every chance to preach to his pupils, or perhaps in some cases to indoctrinate them in Christian precepts. Preaching and indoctrination have no place in any classroom.

The teacher's task is becoming increasingly more difficult and responsible today. Too much is being expected of the schools. At a time of rapid change and uncertainty, society is looking to the teaching profession to provide many of the answers and remedies to social problems, and even sometimes to undertake duties which are not properly inside their sphere. At such a time as this, the perspective and the guidance which Scripture provides are invaluable to any teacher. For we must give our pupils the best things we know and have, and help them to see the choices they in turn must one day make. The Christian teacher must master the Christian principles which the Bible teaches him, and strive to apply them to his particular situation, in the daily round, within his profession, and as a representative of his faith and his profession in the world around him. He might well take as his main maxim a word which Paul wrote to the Colossians (3: 17) when he urged them: 'Whatsoever you do in word or deed, do all in the name of the Lord Jesus Christ.' In a book on New Testament ethics, William Lillie made several points about the grace of God which not only round off this chapter but can well serve as a conclusion to the whole book. He wrote:

'The grace of God . . . is a matter of personal encounter. God, as Person, deals with men as persons. The nearest, although still quite inadequate, analogies of God's dealings in grace with men are a wise parent's dealing with his children or a wise schoolmaster's dealings with his pupils. There is a place for direct commands and prohibitions, and the disobeying of them must produce consequences that teach a lesson, but this kind of thing does not loom too large in a good family or a good school. There is the suggestion given both by word and by example, and this is probably most effective when it is least obvious. There are the opportunities offered, again not too obviously by the wisest parents and teachers, for young people to do and discover things for themselves, and especially for serving others. There are hard tasks to be done, but these are not so hard when the child discovers through them the ready co-operation and understanding of parent or teacher and the strength that comes from fellowship. There is the security which children find in the love of others, and in which they can let themselves go freely in creative activity. There is the growth in wisdom and goodness which comes unconsciously through daily intercourse with the experienced and the good. Those who have had a really great teacher know that what mattered in him was not the knowledge he imparted but that indefinable something which he gave us, we know not how. The good parent or good teacher never asserts his own personality too obviously; otherwise we call him dominating and expect ill effects in the child he is bringing up. We have been describing what a good parent or teacher does for his children, but of course we have been thinking of what God does for us by His grace.'[9]

REFERENCES TO CHAPTER TEN

[1] H. Blamires, *The Christian Mind*, SPCK, 1963, p. 76.
[2] G. Howie, 'St. Augustine's Theory of Christian Education', I, (*Australian*) *Journal of Christian Education*, Vol. V, No. 1, June 1962, p. 27.
[3] S. F. Bayne, Jnr., 'Understanding Europe from the Inside', in E. Fuller, ed., *Schools and Scholarship, The Christian Idea of Education Part II*, Yale University Press, 1962, p. 25.
[4] L. A. Reid, *Philosophy and Education*, Heinemann, 1962, p. 144.
[5] F. E. Gaebelein, *Christian Education in a Democracy*, OUP, 1951, p. 185.
[6] W. R. Niblett, *Christian Education in a Secular Society*, OUP, 1960, p. 123.
[7] John Hansford, 'Pastoral Responsibility . . . I Believe', *Spectrum*, I, ISCF Educational Trust, September 1968, p. 15.
[8] *Ibid.*, p. 13.
[9] W. Lillie, *Studies in New Testament Ethics*, Oliver and Boyd, 1961, p. 40.